SRA Corrective Reading

Decoding A
Word-Attack Basics

A Direct Instruction Program

Siegfried Engelmann

Linda Carnine

Gary Johnson

McGraw Hill Education

Cover Photo: ©Pixtal/age Fotostock

MHEonline.com

Send all inquiries to:
McGraw-Hill Education
8787 Orion Place
Columbus, OH 43240

ISBN: 978-0-07-611204-3
MHID: 0-07-611204-7

Printed in the United States of America.

13 14 15 16 LMN 19 18 17

Contents

Lesson Objectives	LESSON 1 Exercise	LESSON 2 Exercise	LESSON 3 Exercise	LESSON 4 Exercise	LESSON 5 Exercise
Word Attack					
Phonemic Awareness					
Sound/Word Pronunciation	1–4	1–4	2	2, 4, 7	3, 4
Identify Sounds in Words	1, 4	1, 3	3	1, 3, 7	1, 2, 6
Decoding and Word Analysis					
Letter Sounds: *s, a, t, ē, m*	2				
Letter Sounds: *r, ē, t, m, a, s*		2			
Letter Sounds: *d, r, s, ē, a, m, t*			4	4	
Letter Sounds: *i, r, s, ē m, d, a, s*					4
Sounding Out/Blending	5	5	5	5, 6	5
Word Recognition	5	5	5	5, 6	5
Assessment					
Ongoing: Individual Tests	1, 2	1, 2	1, 4	1, 4	1, 4
Formal: Mastery Test				MT 1	
Workbook Exercises					
Decoding and Word Analysis					
Sounding Out/Blending	9	9	7	9	8
Spelling: Sound/Letter Relationships	6	6	6	8	7
Visual Discrimination	7, 8, 10	7, 8, 10	8–10	10–12	9–11
Assessment					
Ongoing: Individual Tests	9	9	7	9	8
Ongoing: Teacher-Monitored Accuracy	11	11	11	14	13
Ongoing: Workcheck	10	10	10	13	12

Please read the *Decoding A Teacher's Guide* before presenting this program.

Note: ‹NEW› indicates the introduction of a new skill or new procedure.

- We're going to do things together. If you all do a good job, everybody in this group will get 6 points.
- You must respond on signal, answer when I give individual turns, follow along when somebody else is reading, and try hard. The group will earn points even if you make mistakes—but everybody must try.
- If the group does not do a good job, nobody will get any points.

WORD-ATTACK SKILLS

═══ EXERCISE 1 ═══
‹NEW› PRONUNCIATIONS: Sounds

Note: Do not write the words on the board. This is an oral exercise.

Task A

1. Listen to the first sound in (pause) **at.** The first sound is ăăă. Say it. (Signal.) ăăă. Yes, ăăă.
2. (Repeat step 1 until firm.)
3. Listen to the last sound in (pause) **at.** The last sound is **t.** Say it. (Signal.) *t.* Yes, **t.**
4. (Repeat step 3 until firm.)

Task B

1. Listen to the first sound in (pause) **see.** The first sound is **sss.** Say it. (Signal.) *sss.* Yes, **sss.**
2. (Repeat step 1 until firm.)
3. Listen to the last sound in (pause) **see.** The last sound is ēēē. Say it. (Signal). *ēēē.* Yes, ēēē.
4. (Repeat step 3 until firm.)

Task C

1. Let's do those sounds again the fast way. Listen: ăăă. Say it. (Signal.) *ăăă.*

2. Listen: **sss.** Say it. (Signal.) *sss.*
3. Listen: **t.** Say it. (Signal.) *t.*
4. Listen: ēēē. Say it. (Signal.) *ēēē.*

Individual test
I'll call on different students to say two sounds. If everybody I call on can say the sounds without making a mistake, we'll go on to the next exercise. (Call on each student to say two sounds. Do not present the same two sounds to each student.)

═══ EXERCISE 2 ═══
‹NEW› SOUND INTRODUCTION

1. My turn. I'll touch these letters and say the sounds.
2. (Point to **s.** Pause. Touch under **s.** Say:) **sss.**
- (Point to **a.** Pause. Touch under **a.** Say:) ăăă.
- (Point to **t.** Pause. Touch under **t.** Say:) **t.**
- (Point to **e.** Pause. Touch under **e.** Say:) ēēē.
- (Point to **m.** Pause. Touch under **m.** Say:) **mmm.**
3. Your turn. Say each sound when I touch it.
4. (Point to **s:**) What sound? (Touch under **s:**) (The students say:) *sss.*
5. (Repeat step 4 for each remaining letter.)

To correct:
a. (Say the sound loudly as soon as you hear an error.)
b. (Point to the sound:) This sound is _____. What sound? (Touch under the letter.)
c. (Repeat the series of letters until all the students can correctly identify all the sounds in order.)

s a t
e m

s a t
e m

Individual test
I'll call on different students to say two sounds. If everybody I call on can say the sounds without making a mistake, we'll go on to the next exercise. (Call on two or three students. Touch under each sound. Each student says all the sounds.)

EXERCISE 3
NEW PRONUNCIATIONS

Task A

1. Listen: **sat.** Say it. (Signal.) *Sat.*
2. Next word: **me.** Say it. (Signal.) *Me.*
3. (Repeat step 2 for **at, eem, eat, am, mă.**)
4. (Repeat all the words until firm.)

Task B Ram, sat, mad

1. I'll say the words that have the sound **ăăă.** What sound? (Signal.) *ăăă.* Yes, **ăăă.**
2. (Repeat step 1 until firm.)
3. Listen: **ram, sat, mad.** Your turn: **ram.** Say it. (Signal.) *Ram.* Yes, **ram.**
4. Next word: **sat.** Say it. (Signal.) *Sat.* Yes, **sat.**
5. Next word: **mad.** Say it. (Signal.) *Mad.* Yes, **mad.**
6. (Repeat steps 3–5 until firm.)
7. (Print on the board:)

> **sat**

• **Sat.** What word? (Signal.) *Sat.* Yes, **sat.**
8. (Touch under **a:**) What's the middle sound in the word **sat?** (Signal.) *ăăă.* Yes, **ăăă.**
9. (Repeat step 8 until firm.)

EXERCISE 4
NEW SAY THE SOUNDS

Note: Do not write the words on the board. This is an oral exercise.

Task A Eat

1. I'm going to say a word slowly without stopping. Then you'll say the word with me.
• First I'll say **ēēēt** slowly. (Hold up a finger for each sound. Do not stop between the two sounds:) **ēēēt.**
2. Everybody, say that with me. Get ready. (Hold up a finger for each sound. Say *ēēēt* with the students.)
3. All by yourselves. Get ready. (Hold up a finger for each sound:) *ēēēt.* (Repeat until the students say the sounds without stopping.)
4. Say it fast. (Signal.) *Eat.*
5. What word? (Signal.) *Eat.* Yes, **eat.**

Task B Am

1. Listen: **ăăămmm.** (Hold up a finger for each sound.)
2. Everybody, say that with me. Get ready. (Hold up a finger for each sound. Say *ăăămmm* with the students.)
3. All by yourselves. Get ready. (Hold up a finger for each sound:) *ăăămmm.*
4. Say it fast. (Signal.) *Am.*
5. What word? (Signal.) *Am.* Yes, **am.**

Task C Ra [ră]

1. Listen: **rrrăăă.** (Hold up a finger for each sound.)
2. Everybody, say that with me. Get ready. (Hold up a finger for each sound. Say *rrrăăă* with the students.)
3. All by yourselves. Get ready. (Hold up a finger for each sound:) *rrrăăă.*
4. Say it fast. (Signal.) *ră.*
5. What word? (Signal.) *ră.* Yes, **ră.** You said the funny word **ră.**

Task D Me

1. Listen: **mmmēēē.** (Hold up a finger for each sound.)
2. Everybody, say that with me. Get ready. (Hold up a finger for each sound. Say *mmmēēē* with the students.)
3. All by yourselves. Get ready. (Hold up a finger for each sound:) *mmmēēē.*
4. Say it fast. (Signal.) *Me.*
5. What word? (Signal.) *Me.* Yes, **me.**

Task E Mat

1. Listen: **mmmăăăt.** (Hold up a finger for each sound.)
2. Everybody, say that with me. Get ready. (Hold up a finger for each sound. Say *mmmăăăt* with the students.)
3. All by yourselves. Get ready. (Hold up a finger for each sound:) *mmmăăăt.*
4. Say it fast. (Signal.) *Mat.*
5. What word? (Signal.) *Mat.* Yes, **mat.**

Task F If

1. Listen: **ĭĭĭfff.** (Hold up a finger for each sound.)
2. Everybody, say that with me. Get ready. (Hold up a finger for each sound. Say *ĭĭĭfff* with the students.)
3. All by yourselves. Get ready. (Hold up a finger for each sound:) *ĭĭĭfff.*
4. Say it fast. (Signal.) *If.*
5. What word? (Signal.) *If.* Yes, **if.**

EXERCISE 5

NEW WORD READING

Task A Eem

1. My turn. I'll say each sound in this word.
- (Point to **ee:**) Two **e**'s together make the sound **ēēē.**
- (Point to **m:**) **mmm.**
2. Your turn. Say each sound when I touch it.
- (Point to **ee:**) What sound? (Touch under **ee:**) *ēēē.*
- (Point to **m:**) What sound? (Touch under **m:**) *mmm.*

3. (Touch the ball of the arrow for **eem:**) Now I'm going to sound out the word. I won't stop between the sounds.
- (Touch under **ee, m** as you say:) **ēēēmmm.**
4. (Touch the ball of the arrow:) Do it with me. Sound it out. Get ready. (Touch under **ee, m:**) *ēēēmmm.* (Repeat until the students say the sounds without pausing.)
5. Again. Sound it out. Get ready. (Touch under **ee, m:**) *ēēēmmm.* (Repeat until firm.)
6. All by yourselves. Sound it out. Get ready. (Touch under **ee, m:**) *ēēēmmm.* (Repeat until firm.)
7. (Touch the ball of the arrow:) Say it fast. (Slash right, along the arrow:) *eem.* Yes, you read the funny word **eem.**

eem

Task B Me

1. Say each sound when I touch it.
- (Point to **m:**) What sound? (Touch under **m:**) *mmm.*
- (Point to **e:**) What sound? (Touch under **e:**) *ēēē.*
2. (Touch the ball of the arrow for **me:**) Now I'm going to sound out the word. I won't stop between the sounds.
- (Touch under **m, e** as you say:) **mmmēēē.**
3. (Touch the ball of the arrow:) Do it with me. Sound it out. Get ready. (Touch under **m, e:**) *mmmēēē.* (Repeat until the students say the sounds without pausing.)
4. Again. Sound it out. Get ready. (Touch under **m, e:**) *mmmēēē.* (Repeat until firm.)
5. All by yourselves. Sound it out. Get ready. (Touch under **m, e:**) *mmmēēē.* (Repeat until firm.)
6. (Touch the ball of the arrow:) Say it fast. (Slash right, along the arrow:) *Me.* Yes, you read the word **me.**

me

Task C Ma [mă]

1. Say each sound when I touch it.
- (Point to **m:**) What sound? (Touch under **m:**) *mmm.*
- (Point to **a:**) What sound? (Touch under **a:**) *ăăă.*

2. (Touch the ball of the arrow for **ma:**) Now I'm going to sound out the word. I won't stop between the sounds.
- (Touch under **m, a** as you say:) **mmmăăă.**

3. (Touch the ball of the arrow:) Do it with me. Sound it out. Get ready. (Touch under **m, a:**) *mmmăăă.* (Repeat until the students say the sounds without pausing.)

4. Again. Sound it out with me. Get ready. (Touch under **m, a:**) *mmmăăă.* (Repeat until firm.)

5. All by yourselves. Sound it out. Get ready. (Touch under **m, a:**) *mmmăăă.* (Repeat until firm.)

6. (Touch the ball of the arrow:) Say it fast. (Slash right, along the arrow:) *mă.* Yes, you read the funny word **mă.**

ma

NEW Task D Am

1. (Point to **a:**) What sound? (Touch under **a:**) *ăăă.*

2. (Point to **m:**) What sound? (Touch under **m:**) *mmm.*

3. (Touch the ball of the arrow:) My turn to sound out this word.
- (Touch under **a, m** as you say:) **ăăămmm.** (Do not pause between the sounds.)

4. (Touch the ball of the arrow:) Your turn. Sound it out. Get ready. (Touch under **a, m:**) *ăăămmm.* (Repeat until the students say the sounds without pausing.)

To correct:
a. My turn to sound it out. I won't stop between the sounds. (Touch under each letter or combination. Say the sounds without pausing between them.)
b. Sound it out with me. Get ready. (Touch under each sound as you and the students say the sounds without pausing between them.)
c. Again. (Repeat step *b* until firm.)
d. (Repeat step 4 until firm.)

5. (Touch the ball of the arrow:) Say it fast. (Slash right, along the arrow:) *Am.* Yes, **am.**

am

Task E At

1. (Point to **a:**) What sound? (Touch under **a:**) *ăăă.*

2. (Point to **t:**) What sound? (Touch under **t:**) *t.*

3. (Touch the ball of the arrow:) My turn to sound out this word.
- (Touch under **a, t** as you say:) **ăăăt.** (Do not pause between the sounds.)

4. (Touch the ball of the arrow:) Your turn. Sound it out. Get ready. (Touch under **a, t.**) *ăăăt.* (Repeat until the students say the sounds without pausing.)

5. (Touch the ball of the arrow:) Say it fast. (Slash right, along the arrow:) *At.* Yes, **at.**

at

Task F Eet

1. (Point to **ee:**) What sound? (Touch under **ee:**) ēēē.
2. (Point to **t:**) What sound? (Touch under **t.**) t.
3. (Touch the ball of the arrow:)
   My turn to sound out this funny word.
   • (Touch under **ee, t** as you say:) ēēēt.
   (Do not pause between the sounds.)
4. (Touch the ball of the arrow:) Your turn.
   Sound it out. Get ready. (Touch under
   ee, t:) ēēēt. (Repeat until the students say
   the sounds without pausing.)
5. (Touch the ball of the arrow:) Say it fast.
   (Slash right, along the arrow:) eet. Yes, **eet.**

WORKBOOK EXERCISES

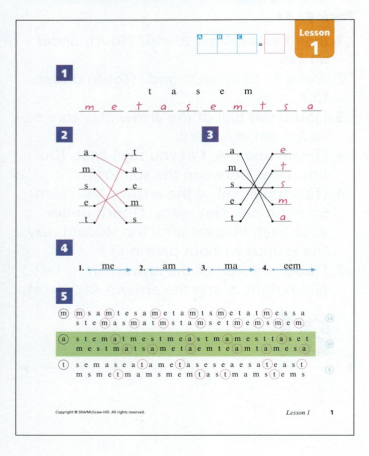

Note: Pass out the Workbooks. Direct the students to open their Workbooks to Lesson 1.

• (If the group worked well during the word attack, say:) Everybody, write 6 in Box A at the top of your Workbook lesson. That shows that the group earned 6 points today.
• (If the group did **not** work well during the word attack, say:) You did not earn any group points today, but everybody will get a chance to earn points on the Workbook lesson.
• Now we're going to do exercises in the Workbook. You can earn up to 8 points for these activities.
• If you do a good job on your Workbook and make 0 or 1 error, you can earn 8 points. How many points can you earn? (Signal.) 8.
• If you make 2 or 3 errors, you can still earn 3 points.

━━━━━━━━ **EXERCISE 6** ━━━━━━━━
NEW **SOUND DICTATION**

1. Everybody, touch part 1 in your Workbook. ✓
• These are the sounds you did before. Say all the sounds once more before you write the letters.
2. Touch the first sound. ✓
• What sound? (Clap.) t. Yes, **t.**
3. Touch the next sound. ✓
• What sound? (Clap.) ăăă. Yes, **ăăă.**
4. (Repeat step 3 for **sss, ēēē, mmm.**)
5. Now you're going to write the letters for the sounds I say. First sound. (Pause.) **mmm.** What sound? (Clap.) mmm.
• Write it in the first blank. (Observe students and give feedback.)
6. Next sound. (Pause.) ēēē. What sound? (Clap.) ēēē.
• Write it in the next blank. (Observe students and give feedback.)

7. (Repeat step 6 for **t, ăăă, sss, ēēē, mmm, t, sss, ăăă**.)
8. (Check that students can write all the letters without errors.)

=== **EXERCISE 7** ===

NEW **MATCHING SOUNDS**

1. Everybody, touch part 2. ✓
- This is a matching exercise. You're going to match the letters in the first column with the letters in the second column.
2. When I clap, you say the sounds of the letters in the first column. Touch the first letter. ✓
- What sound? (Clap.) *ăăă*.
3. Touch the next letter. ✓
- What sound? (Clap.) *mmm*.
4. (Repeat step 3 for **s, ē, t**.)
5. (Repeat the sounds until firm.)
6. Everybody, touch **ăăă** in the first column. ✓
- Draw a line from the ball of that **ăăă** to the ball of **ăăă** in the second column. ✓
7. Everybody, touch **mmm** in the first column. ✓
- Draw a line from the ball of **mmm** to the ball of **mmm** in the second column.
(Observe students and give feedback.)
8. Do the rest of the letters on your own. Now.
(Observe students and give feedback.)

=== **EXERCISE 8** ===

NEW **MATCHING AND COPYING SOUNDS**

1. Everybody, touch part 3. ✓
- This is another matching exercise. Follow the line from each letter in the first column. Write the letter in the blank.
2. Everybody, follow the line from **ăăă** and show me where you're going to write the other **ăăă**. ✓
3. Write **ăăă** in the correct blank.
(Observe students and give feedback.)
4. Follow the line from **mmm** and show me where you're going to write the other **mmm**. ✓
5. Write **mmm** in the correct blank.
(Observe students and give feedback.)

6. Write the rest of the letters on your own. Now.
(Observe students and give feedback.)

=== **EXERCISE 9** ===

NEW **SOUND IT OUT: Workbook**

1. Everybody, touch part 4. ✓
- These are some of the words we sounded out earlier. This time, you're going to touch the letters and sound out the words.
2. Touch the ball of the arrow for word 1. ✓
3. Sound it out. Get ready. (Clap for **m, e:**) *mmmēēē*. (Repeat until the students say the sounds without pausing.)

To correct:
a. My turn to sound it out. I won't stop between the sounds. Touch the letters as I say the sounds. Get ready. (Clap for **m, e** as you say:) **mmmēēē**.
b. Your turn to sound it out. Get ready. (Clap for **m, e:**) *mmmēēē*.
c. Again. (Repeat step 3.)

4. Touch the ball of the arrow for word 2. ✓
5. Sound it out. Get ready. (Clap for **a, m:**) *ăăămmm*. (Repeat until the students say the sounds without pausing.)
6. Touch the ball of the arrow for word 3. ✓
7. Sound it out. Get ready. (Clap for **m, a:**) *mmmăăă*. (Repeat until the students say the sounds without pausing.)
8. Touch the ball of the arrow for word 4. ✓
9. Sound it out. Get ready. (Clap for **ee, m:**) *ēēēmmm*. (Repeat until the students say the sounds without pausing.)

Individual test
(Call on each student to sound out two words.) Sound out the word. Remember, touch the sounds as you say them. Don't stop between the sounds.

EXERCISE 10
NEW **CIRCLE GAME**

1. Everybody, touch part 5. ✓
- The circled letter at the beginning of each line tells you what to circle in that line.
2. The number at the end of the line tells how many there are.
3. Touch the circled letter at the beginning of the first line. ✓
- What sound? (Clap.) *mmm.*
  Yes, **mmm.** You'll circle every **mmm** in those two lines.
- How many are there? (Clap.) *14.*
4. Touch the next circled letter. ✓
- What sound? (Clap.) *ăăă.*
  Yes, **ăăă.** You'll circle every **ăăă** in those two lines.
- How many are there? (Clap.) *10.*
5. Touch the next circled letter. ✓
- What sound? (Clap.) *t.*
  Yes, **t.** You'll circle every **t** in those two lines.
- How many are there? (Clap.) *8.*
6. See how many lines you can do without making a mistake.
  (Observe students and give feedback.)

Note: Record points in Box B for each student's performance on assigned Workbook activities.

0–1 error	8 points
2–3 errors	3 points
4 or more errors	0 points

INDIVIDUAL READING CHECKOUTS

EXERCISE 11
NEW **SOUND-IT-OUT CHECKOUT**

- Practice sounding out all the words in part 4 without stopping between sounds. You'll each get a turn to sound out all these words. You can earn as many as 6 points for this reading.
- If you sound out all the words with no more than 1 error, you'll earn 6 points.
- If you make more than 1 error, you do not earn any points. But you'll have another chance to earn 6 points by studying the words some more and reading them again.
- (Check the students individually.)
- (Record either 6 or 0 points in Box C.)

Lesson point total

(Tell students to add the points in Boxes A, B, and C and to write this total in the last box at the top of the Workbook page. Maximum for the lesson = 20 points.)

Point Summary Chart

(Tell students to write this point total in the box for Lesson 1 in the Point Summary Chart, which is on the inside front cover of the Workbook.)

END OF LESSON 1

WORD-ATTACK SKILLS

Remember, you can earn 6 points if everybody in the group responds on signal, follows along when somebody else is reading, and tries hard.

═══════ **EXERCISE 1** ═══════

NEW **PRONUNCIATIONS: Sounds**

> **Note:** Do not write the words on the board. This is an oral exercise.

Task A

1. Listen to the first sound in (pause) **if.** The first sound is ĭĭĭ. Say it. (Signal.) *ĭĭĭ.* Yes, **ĭĭĭ.**
2. (Repeat step 1 until firm.)
3. Listen to the last sound in (pause) **if.** The last sound is **fff.** Say it. (Signal.) *fff.* Yes, **fff.**
4. (Repeat step 3 until firm.)

Task B

1. Listen to the first sound in (pause) **reed.** The first sound is **rrr.** Say it. (Signal.) *rrr.* Yes, **rrr.**
2. (Repeat step 1 until firm.)
3. Listen to the middle sound in (pause) **reed.** The middle sound is ēēē. Say it. (Signal.) *ēēē.* Yes, **ēēē.**
4. (Repeat step 3 until firm.)
5. Listen to the last sound in (pause) **reed.** The last sound is **d.** Say it. (Signal.) *d.* Yes, **d.** (Repeat until firm.)

Task C

1. New word. Listen to the first sound in (pause) **ask.** The first sound is ăăă. Say it. (Signal.) *ăăă.* Yes, **ăăă.**
2. (Repeat step 1 until firm.)
3. Listen to the middle sound in (pause) **ask.** The middle sound is **sss.** Say it. (Signal.) *sss.* Yes, **sss.**
4. (Repeat step 3 until firm.)
5. Listen to the last sound in (pause) **ask.** The last sound is **k.** Say it. (Signal.) *k.* Yes, **k.**
6. (Repeat step 5 until firm.)

Task D

1. Let's do those sounds again the fast way. Listen: ĭĭĭ. Say it. (Signal.) *ĭĭĭ.*
2. Listen: **ēēē.** Say it. (Signal.) *ēēē.*
3. Listen: **rrr.** Say it. (Signal.) *rrr.*
4. Listen: **k.** Say it. (Signal.) *k.*
5. Listen: **sss.** Say it. (Signal.) *sss.*
6. Listen: **ăăă.** Say it. (Signal.) *ăăă.*

> **Individual test**
> (Call on different students to say two sounds. Do not present the same sounds to each student.)

═══════ **EXERCISE 2** ═══════

NEW **SOUND INTRODUCTION**

1. (Point to **r:**) This letter makes the sound **rrr.** (Pause.) What sound? (Touch under **r:**) *rrr.* Yes, **rrr.**
2. My turn. I'll touch these letters and say the sounds.
3. (Point to **r.** Pause. Touch under **r.** Say:) **rrr.**
• (Point to **e.** Pause. Touch under **e.** Say:) **ēēē.**
• (Point to **t.** Pause. Touch under **t.** Say:) **t.**
• (Point to **m.** Pause. Touch under **m.** Say:) **mmm.**
• (Point to **a.** Pause. Touch under **a.** Say:) **ăăă.**
• (Point to **s.** Pause. Touch under **s.** Say:) **sss.**

r e t
m a s

4. Your turn. Say each sound when I touch it.
5. (Point to **r**:) What sound? (Touch under **r**:) (The students say:) *rrr.*
6. (Repeat step 5 for each remaining letter.)

To correct:
a. (Say the sound loudly as soon as you hear an error.)
b. (Point to the sound:) This sound is _____. What sound? (Touch under the letter.)
c. (Repeat the series of letters until all the students can correctly identify all the sounds in order.)

r e t
m a s

Individual test
I'll call on different students to say all the sounds. If everybody I call on can say all the sounds without making a mistake, we'll go on to the next exercise. (Call on two or three students. Touch under each sound. Each student says all the sounds.)

EXERCISE 3
PRONUNCIATIONS

Task A
1. Listen: She was **sad.** (Pause.) **Sad.** Say it. (Signal.) *Sad.*
2. Next word. Listen: She **sat** on a chair. (Pause.) **Sat.** Say it. (Signal.) *Sat.*
3. Next word: **fan.** Say it. (Signal.) *Fan.*
4. (Repeat step 3 for **fin, is, mat, sam, ram, am, să.** Repeat all the words until firm.)

Task B Seat, me, meet
1. I'll say words that have the sound **ēēē.** What sound? (Signal.) *ēēē.* Yes, **ēēē.**
2. (Repeat step 1 until firm.)

3. Listen: **seat, me, meet.** Your turn: **seat.** Say it. (Signal.) *Seat.* Yes, **seat.**
4. Next word: **me.** Say it. (Signal.) *Me.* Yes, **me.**
5. Next word: **meet.** Say it. (Signal.) *Meet.* Yes, **meet.**
6. (Repeat steps 3–5 until firm.)
7. (Print on the board:)

meet

• **What word?** (Signal.) *Meet.* Yes, **meet.**
8. (Touch under **ee**:) What's the middle sound in the word **meet?** (Signal.) *ēēē.* Yes, **ēēē.**
9. (Repeat step 8 until firm.)

EXERCISE 4
SAY THE SOUNDS

Note: Do not write the words on the board. This is an oral exercise.

Task A Eat
1. I'm going to say a word slowly without stopping. Then you'll say the word with me.
• First I'll say **ēēēt** slowly. (Hold up a finger for each sound. Do not stop between the sounds.) **ēēēt.**
2. Everybody, say that with me. Get ready. (Hold up a finger for each sound. Say *ēēēt* with the students.)
3. All by yourselves. Get ready. (Hold up a finger for each sound.) *ēēēt.* (Repeat until the students say the sounds without stopping.)
4. Say it fast. (Signal.) *Eat.*
5. What word? (Signal.) *Eat.* Yes, **eat.**

Task B Is
1. Listen: **ĭĭĭzzz.** (Hold up a finger for each sound.)
2. Everybody, say that with me. Get ready. (Hold up a finger for each sound. Say *ĭĭĭzzz* with the students.)

3. All by yourselves. Get ready. (Hold up a finger for each sound.) ĭĭĭzzz.

4. Say it fast. (Signal.) *Is.*

5. What word? (Signal.) *Is.* Yes, **is.**

Task C Fan

1. Listen: **fffăăănnn.** (Hold up a finger for each sound.)

2. Everybody, say that with me. Get ready. (Hold up a finger for each sound. Say *fffăăănnn* with the students.)

3. All by yourselves. Get ready. (Hold up a finger for each sound.) *fffăăănnn.*

4. Say it fast. (Signal.) *Fan.*

5. What word? (Signal.) *Fan.* Yes, **fan.**

Task D See

1. Listen: **sssēēē.** (Hold up a finger for each sound.)

2. Everybody, say that with me. Get ready. (Hold up a finger for each sound. Say *sssēēē* with the students.)

3. All by yourselves. Get ready. (Hold up a finger for each sound.) *sssēēē.*

4. Say it fast. (Signal.) *See.*

5. What word? (Signal.) *See.* Yes, **see.**

Task E If

1. Listen: **ĭĭĭfff.** (Hold up a finger for each sound.)

2. Everybody, say that with me. Get ready. (Hold up a finger for each sound. Say *ĭĭĭfff* with the students.)

3. All by yourselves. Get ready. (Hold up a finger for each sound.) *ĭĭĭfff.*

4. Say it fast. (Signal.) *If.*

5. What word? (Signal.) *If.* Yes, **if.**

Task F Ram

1. Listen: **rrrăăămmm.** (Hold up a finger for each sound.)

2. Everybody, say that with me. Get ready. (Hold up a finger for each sound. Say *rrrăăămmm* with the students.)

3. All by yourselves. Get ready. (Hold up a finger for each sound.) *rrrăăămmm.*

4. Say it fast. (Signal.) *Ram.*

5. What word? (Signal.) *Ram.* Yes, **ram.**

EXERCISE 5
NEW WORD READING

Task A Me

1. Say each sound when I touch it.

- (Point to **m:**) What sound? (Touch under **m:**) *mmm.*

- (Point to **e:**) What sound? (Touch under **e:**) *ēēē.*

2. (Touch the ball of the arrow for **me:**) Now I'm going to sound out the word. I won't stop between the sounds.

- (Touch under **m, e** as you say:) **mmmēēē.**

3. (Touch the ball of the arrow:) Do it with me. Sound it out. Get ready. (Touch under **m, e:**) **mmmēēē.** (Repeat until the students say the sounds without pausing.)

4. Again. Sound it out. Get ready. (Touch under **m, e:**) **mmmēēē.** (Repeat until firm.)

5. All by yourselves. Sound it out. Get ready. (Touch under **m, e:**) *mmmēēē.* (Repeat until firm.)

6. (Touch the ball of the arrow:) Say it fast. (Slash right, along the arrow.) *Me.* Yes, you read the word **me.**

me

Task B See

1. Say each sound when I touch it.

- (Point to **s:**) What sound? (Touch under **s:**) *sss.*

- (Point to **ee:**) What sound? (Touch under **ee:**) *ēēē.*

2. (Touch the ball of the arrow for **see:**) Now I'm going to sound out the word. I won't stop between the sounds.

- (Touch under **s, ee** as you say:) **sssēēē.**

see

3. (Touch the ball of the arrow:) Do it with me. Sound it out. Get ready. (Touch under **s, ee:**) *sssēēē.* (Repeat until the students say the sounds without pausing.)

4. Again. Sound it out. Get ready. (Touch under **s, ee:**) *sssēēē.* (Repeat until firm.)

5. All by yourselves. Sound it out. Get ready. (Touch under **s, ee:**) *sssēēē.* (Repeat until firm.)

6. (Touch the ball of the arrow:) Say it fast. (Slash right, along the arrow:) *See.* Yes, you read the word **see.**

see

→

Task C Sa [să]

1. Say each sound when I touch it.
- (Point to **s:**) What sound? (Touch under **s:**) *sss.*
- (Point to **a:**) What sound? (Touch under **a:**) *ăăă.*

2. (Touch the ball of the arrow for **sa:**) Now I'm going to sound out the word. I won't stop between the sounds.
- (Touch under **s, a** as you say:) **sssăăă.**

3. (Touch the ball of the arrow:) Do it with me. Sound it out. Get ready. (Touch under **s, a:**) *sssăăă.* (Repeat until the students say the sounds without pausing.)

4. Again. Sound it out. Get ready. (Touch under **s, a:**) *sssăăă.* (Repeat until firm.)

5. All by yourselves. Sound it out. Get ready. (Touch under **s, a:**) *sssăăă.* (Repeat until firm.)

6. (Touch the ball of the arrow:) Say it fast. (Slash right, along the arrow:) *să.* Yes, you read the funny word **să.**

sa

→

Task D Eem

1. (Point to **ee:**) What sound? (Touch under **ee:**) *ēēē.*

2. (Point to **m:**) What sound? (Touch under **m:**) *mmm.*

3. (Touch the ball of the arrow:) My turn to sound out this funny word.
- (Touch under **ee, m** as you say:) **ēēēmmm.** (Do not pause between sounds.)

4. (Touch the ball of the arrow:) Your turn. Sound it out. Get ready. (Touch under **ee, m:**) *ēēēmmm.* (Repeat until the students say the sounds without pausing.)

> **To correct:**
> a. My turn to sound it out. I won't stop between the sounds. (Touch under each letter or combination. Say the sounds without pausing between them.)
> b. Sound it out with me. Get ready. (Touch under each sound as you and the students say the sounds without pausing.)
> c. Again. (Repeat step *b* until firm.)
> d. (Repeat step 4 until firm.)

5. (Touch the ball of the arrow:) Say it fast. (Slash right, along the arrow:) *eem.* Yes, **eem.**

eem

→

Task E At

1. (Point to **a**:) What sound? (Touch under **a**:) *ăăă.*
2. (Point to **t**:) What sound? (Touch under **t**:) *t.*
3. (Touch the ball of the arrow:) My turn to sound out this word.
- (Touch under **a, t** as you say:) *ăăăt.* (Do not pause between the sounds.)
4. (Touch the ball of the arrow:) Your turn. Sound it out. Get ready. (Touch under **a, t**:) *ăăăt.* (Repeat until the students say the sounds without pausing.)
5. (Touch the ball of the arrow:) Say it fast. (Slash right, along the arrow:) *At.* Yes, **at.**

Task F Eet

1. (Point to **ee**:) What sound? (Touch under **ee**:) *ēēē.*
2. (Point to **t**:) What sound? (Touch under **t**:) *t.*
3. (Touch the ball of the arrow:) My turn to sound out this word.
- (Touch under **ee, t** as you say:) *ēēēt.* (Do not pause between the sounds.)
4. (Touch the ball of the arrow:) Your turn. Sound it out. Get ready. (Touch under **ee, t**:) *ēēēt.* (Repeat until the students say the sounds without pausing.)
5. (Touch the ball of the arrow:) Say it fast. (Slash right, along the arrow:) *eet.* Yes, **eet.**

Task G Ree

1. (Point to **r**:) What sound? (Touch under **r**:) *rrr.*
2. (Point to **ee**:) What sound? (Touch under **ee**:) *ēēē.*
3. (Touch the ball of the arrow:) My turn to sound out this word.
- (Touch under **r, ee** as you say:) *rrrēēē.* (Do not pause between the sounds.)
4. (Touch the ball of the arrow.) Your turn. Sound it out. Get ready. (Touch under **r, ee**:) *rrrēēē.* (Repeat until the students say the sounds without pausing.)
5. (Touch the ball of the arrow:) Say it fast. (Slash right, along the arrow:) *ree.* Yes, **ree.** You read the funny word **ree.**

ree ⟶

Task H Ra

1. (Point to **r**:) What sound? (Touch under **r**:) *rrr.*
2. (Point to **a**:) What sound? (Touch under **a**:) *ăăă.*
3. (Touch the ball of the arrow:) My turn to sound out this word.
- (Touch under **r, a** as you say:) *rrrăăă.* (Do not pause between the sounds.)
4. (Touch the ball of the arrow:) Your turn. Sound it out. Get ready. (Touch under **r, a**:) *rrrăăă.* (Repeat until the students say the sounds without pausing.)
5. (Touch the ball of the arrow:) Say it fast. (Slash right, along the arrow:) *ră.* Yes, **ră.** Yes, you read the funny word **ră.**

ra ⟶

WORKBOOK EXERCISES

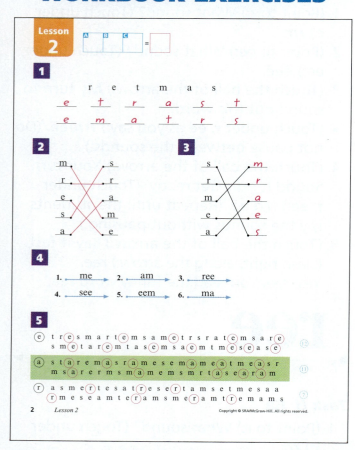

Note: Pass out the Workbooks. Direct the students to open their Workbooks to Lesson 2.

- (If the group worked well during the word attack, say:) Everybody, write 6 in Box A at the top of your Workbook lesson. That shows that the group earned 6 points today.
- (If the group did **not** work well during the word attack, say:) You did not earn any group points today, but everybody will get a chance to earn points on the Workbook lesson.
- Now we're going to do exercises in the Workbook. You can earn up to 8 points for these activities.

━━━━━━━━━━━━━━ **EXERCISE 6** ━━━━━━━━━━━━━━

SOUND DICTATION

1. Everybody, touch part 1 in your Workbook. ✓
- These are the sounds you did before. Say all the sounds once more before you write the letters.
2. Touch the first sound. ✓
- What sound? (Clap.) *rrr.* Yes, **rrr.**
3. Touch the next sound. ✓
- What sound? (Clap.) *ēēē.* Yes, **ēēē.**
4. (Repeat step 3 for **t, mmm, ăăă, sss.**)
5. Now you're going to write the letters for the sounds I say. First sound. (Pause.) **ēēē.** What sound? (Clap.) *ēēē.*
- Write it in the first blank. (Observe students and give feedback.)
6. Next sound. (Pause.) **t.** What sound? (Clap.) *t.*
- Write it in the next blank. (Observe students and give feedback.)
7. (Repeat step 6 for **rrr, ăăă, sss, t, ēēē, mmm, ăăă, t, rrr, sss.**)
8. (Check that students can write all the letters without errors.)

━━━━━━━━━━━━━━ **EXERCISE 7** ━━━━━━━━━━━━━━

MATCHING SOUNDS

1. Everybody, touch part 2. ✓
- This is a matching exercise. You're going to match the letters in the first column with the letters in the second column.
2. When I clap, you say the sounds of the letters in the first column. Touch the first letter. ✓
- What sound? (Clap.) *mmm.*
3. Touch the next letter. ✓
- What sound? (Clap.) *rrr.*
4. (Repeat step 3 for **ē, s, ă.**)
5. (Repeat the sounds until firm.)
6. Everybody, touch **mmm** in the first column. ✓
- Draw a line from the ball of that **mmm** to the ball of **mmm** in the second column. (Observe students and give feedback.)

7. Everybody, touch **rrr** in the first column. ✓
- Draw a line from the ball of that **rrr** to the ball of **rrr** in the second column. (Observe students and give feedback.)
8. Do the rest of the letters on your own. Now. (Observe students and give feedback.)

EXERCISE 8
MATCHING AND COPYING SOUNDS

1. Everybody, touch part 3. ✓
- This is another matching exercise. Follow the line from each letter in the first column. Write the letter in the blank.
2. Everybody, follow the line from **sss** and show me where you're going to write the other **sss**. ✓
3. Write **sss** in the correct blank. (Observe students and give feedback.)
4. Follow the line from **rrr** and show me where you're going to write the other **rrr**. ✓
5. Write **rrr** in the correct blank. (Observe students and give feedback.)
6. Write the rest of the letters on your own. Now. (Observe students and give feedback.)

EXERCISE 9
SOUND IT OUT: Workbook

1. Everybody, touch part 4. ✓
- These are some of the words we sounded out earlier. This time, you're going to touch the letters and sound out the words.
2. Touch the ball of the arrow for word 1. ✓
3. Sound it out. Get ready. (Clap for **m, e**:) *mmmēēē.* (Repeat until the students say the sounds without pausing.)

To correct:
a. My turn to sound it out. I won't stop between the sounds. Touch the letters as I say the sounds. Get ready. (Clap for **m, e** as you say:) **mmmēēē.**
b. Your turn to sound it out. Get ready. (Clap for **m, e**:) *mmmēēē.*
c. Again. (Repeat step 3.)

4. Touch the ball of the arrow for word 2. ✓
5. Sound it out. Get ready. (Clap for **a, m**:) *ăăămmm.* (Repeat until the students say the sounds without pausing.)
6. Touch the ball of the arrow for word 3. ✓
7. Sound it out. Get ready. (Clap for **r, ee**:) *rrrēēē.* (Repeat until the students say the sounds without pausing.)
8. Touch the ball of the arrow for word 4. ✓
9. Sound it out. Get ready. (Clap for **s, ee**:) *sssēēē.* (Repeat until the students say the sounds without pausing.)
10. Touch the ball of the arrow for word 5. ✓
11. Sound it out. Get ready. (Clap for **ee, m**:) *ēēēmmm.* (Repeat until the students say the sounds without pausing.)
12. Touch the ball of the arrow for word 6. ✓
13. Sound it out. Get ready. (Clap for **m, a**:) *mmmăăă.* (Repeat until the students say the sounds without pausing.)

Individual test
(Call on each student to sound out two words.) Sound out the word. Remember, touch the sounds as you say them. Don't stop between the sounds.

EXERCISE 10
CIRCLE GAME

1. Everybody, touch part 5. ✓
- The circled letter at the beginning of each line tells you what to circle in that line.
2. The number at the end of the line tells how many there are.
3. Touch the circled letter at the beginning of the first line. ✓
- What sound? (Clap.) *ēēē.* Yes, **ēēē.** You'll circle every **ēēē** in those two lines.
- How many are there? (Clap.) *12.*
4. Touch the next circled letter. ✓
- What sound? (Clap.) *ăăă.* Yes, **ăăă.** You'll circle every **ăăă** in those two lines.
- How many are there? (Clap.) *11.*

5. Touch the next circled letter. ✓
- What sound? (Clap.) *rrr.*
  Yes, **rrr.** You'll circle every **rrr** in those two lines.
- How many are there? (Clap.) *7.*
6. See how many lines you can do without making a mistake.
   (Observe students and give feedback.)

> **Note:** Record points in Box B for each student's performance on assigned Workbook activities.
> | | |
> |---|---|
> | 0–1 error | 8 points |
> | 2–3 errors | 3 points |
> | 4 or more errors | 0 points |

INDIVIDUAL READING CHECKOUTS

EXERCISE 11
SOUND-IT-OUT CHECKOUT

- Practice sounding out all the words in part 4 without stopping between sounds. You'll each get a turn to sound out all these words. You can earn as many as 6 points for this reading.
- If you sound out all the words with no more than 1 error, you'll earn 6 points.
- If you make more than 1 error, you do not earn any points. But you'll have another chance to earn 6 points by studying the words some more and reading them again.
- (Check the students individually.)
- (Record either 6 or 0 points in Box C.)

Lesson point total
(Tell students to add the points in Boxes A, B, and C and to write this total in the last box at the top of the Workbook page. Maximum for the lesson = 20 points.)

Point Summary Chart
(Tell students to write this point total in the box for Lesson 2 in the Point Summary Chart, which is on the inside front cover of the Workbook.)

END OF LESSON 2

WORD-ATTACK SKILLS

Remember, you can earn 6 points if everybody in the group responds on signal, follows along when somebody else is reading, and tries hard.

━━━━━ **EXERCISE 1** ━━━━━

PRONUNCIATIONS: Sounds

> **Note:** Do not write the words on the board. This is an oral exercise.

Task A

1. Listen to the first sound in (pause) **seed.** The first sound is **sss.** Say it. (Signal.) *sss.* Yes, **sss.**
2. (Repeat step 1 until firm.)
3. Listen to the middle sound in (pause) **seed.** The middle sound is **ēēē.** Say it. (Signal.) *ēēē.* Yes, **ēēē.**
4. (Repeat step 3 until firm.)
5. Listen to the last sound in (pause) **seed.** The last sound is **d.** Say it. (Signal.) *d.* Yes, **d.**
6. (Repeat step 5 until firm.)

Task B

1. Listen to the first sound in (pause) **it.** The first sound is **ĭĭĭ.** Say it. (Signal.) *ĭĭĭ.* Yes, **ĭĭĭ.**
2. (Repeat step 1 until firm.)
3. Listen to the last sound in (pause) **it.** The last sound is **t.** Say it. (Signal.) *t.* Yes, **t.**
4. (Repeat step 3 until firm.)

Task C

1. New word. Listen to the first sound in (pause) **ram.** The first sound is **rrr.** Say it. (Signal.) *rrr.* Yes, **rrr.** (Repeat until firm.)
2. Listen to the middle sound in (pause) **ram.** The middle sound is **ăăă.** Say it. (Signal.) *ăăă.* Yes, **ăăă.** (Repeat until firm.)
3. Listen to the last sound in (pause) **ram.** The last sound is **mmm.** Say it. (Signal.) *mmm.* Yes, **mmm.** (Repeat until firm.)

Task D

1. Let's do those sounds again the fast way. Listen: **mmm.** Say it. (Signal.) *mmm.*
2. Listen: **ĭĭĭ.** Say it. (Signal.) *ĭĭĭ.*

3. Listen: **d.** Say it. (Signal.) *d.*
4. Listen: **ēēē.** Say it. (Signal.) *ēēē.*
5. Listen: **sss.** Say it. (Signal.) *sss.*
6. Listen: **ăăă.** Say it. (Signal.) *ăăă.*
7. Listen: **t.** Say it. (Signal.) *t.*
8. Listen: **rrr.** Say it. (Signal.) *rrr.*

> **Individual test**
> (Call on different students to say two sounds. Do not present the same two sounds to each student.)

━━━━━ **EXERCISE 2** ━━━━━

PRONUNCIATIONS

> **Note:** Do not write the words on the board. This is an oral exercise.

Task A

1. Listen. She had a **sack.** (Pause.) **Sack.** Say it. (Signal.) *Sack.*
2. Next word: **reem.** Say it. (Signal.) *Reem.*
3. (Repeat step 2 for **rat, fan.**)
4. (Repeat all the words until firm.)

Task B Sad, sat, mad

1. I'll say words that have the sound **ăăă.** What sound? (Signal.) *ăăă.* Yes, **ăăă.**
2. (Repeat step 1 until firm.)
3. Listen: **sad, sat, mad.** Your turn: **sad.** Say it. (Signal.) *Sad.* Yes, **sad.**
4. Next word: **sat.** Say it. (Signal.) *Sat.* Yes, **sat.**
5. Next word: **mad.** Say it. (Signal.) *Mad.* Yes, **mad.**
6. (Repeat steps 3–5 until firm.)
7. (Print on the board:)

> **mad**

- What word? (Signal.) *Mad.* Yes, **mad.**
8. (Touch under **a:**) What's the middle sound in the word **mad?** (Signal.) *ăăă.* Yes, **ăăă.**
9. (Repeat step 8 until firm.)

d r s

r e a

m t

EXERCISE 3

NEW SAY THE SOUNDS

Note: Do not write the words on the board. This is an oral exercise.

1. First you're going to say a word slowly without stopping between the sounds. Then you're going to say the word fast.
2. Listen: ăăăt. (Hold up a finger for each sound.)
3. Say the sounds in (pause) ăăăt. Get ready. (Hold up a finger for each sound.) *ăăăt.* (Repeat until the students say the sounds without stopping.)
4. Say it fast. (Signal.) *At.*
5. What word? (Signal.) *At.* Yes, **at.**
6. (Repeat steps 2–5 for **an, am, eat, meet, fish, it, fan, if, see.**)

Individual test
I'll call on different students to say all the sounds. If everybody I call on can say all the sounds without making a mistake, we'll go on to the next exercise. (Call on two or three students. Touch under each sound. Each student says all the sounds.)

EXERCISE 4

SOUND INTRODUCTION

1. (Point to **d:**) This letter makes the sound **d.** (Pause.) What sound? (Touch under **d:**) *d.* Yes, **d.**
2. (Point to **r:**) This letter makes the sound **rrr.** (Pause.) What sound? (Touch under **r:**) *rrr.* Yes, **rrr.**
3. Say each sound when I touch it.
4. (Point to **d:**) What sound? (Touch under **d:**) *d.*
5. (Repeat step 4 for **s, r, ē, ă, m, t.**)

To correct:
a. (Say the sound loudly as soon as you hear an error.)
b. (Point to the sound:) This sound is _____. What sound? (Touch.)
c. (Repeat the series of letters until all the students can correctly identify all the sounds in order.)

EXERCISE 5

WORD READING

Task A Ees

1. Say each sound when I touch it.
- (Point to **ee:**) What sound? (Touch under **ee:**) *ēēē.*
- (Point to **s:**) What sound? (Touch under **s:**) *sss.*
2. (Touch the ball of the arrow for **ees:**) Now I'm going to sound out the word. I won't stop between the sounds.
- (Touch under **ee, s** as you say:) **ēēēsss.**
3. (Touch the ball of the arrow:) Do it with me. Sound it out. Get ready. (Touch under **ee, s:**) *ēēēsss.* (Repeat until the students say the sounds without pausing.)
4. Again. Sound it out. Get ready. (Touch under **ee, s:**) *ēēēsss.* (Repeat until firm.)
5. All by yourselves. Sound it out. Get ready. (Touch under **ee, s:**) *ēēēsss.* (Repeat until firm.)

ees ————————————————→

6. (Touch the ball of the arrow:) Say it fast. (Slash right, along the arrow:) *ees.* Yes, you read the funny word **ees.**

ees

Task B Ra [rǎ]

1. Say each sound when I touch it.
- (Point to **r**:) What sound? (Touch under **r**:) *rrr.*
- (Point to **a**:) What sound? (Touch under **a**:) *ǎǎǎ.*
2. (Touch the ball of the arrow for **ra**:) Now I'm going to sound out the word. I won't stop between the sounds.
- (Touch under **r, a** as you say:) **rrrǎǎǎ.**
3. (Touch the ball of the arrow:) Do it with me. Sound it out. Get ready. (Touch under **r, a**:) *rrrǎǎǎ.* (Repeat until the students say the sounds without pausing.)
4. Again. Sound it out. Get ready. (Touch under **r, a**:) *rrrǎǎǎ.* (Repeat until firm.)
5. All by yourselves. Sound it out. Get ready. (Touch under **r, a**:) *rrrǎǎǎ.* (Repeat until firm.)
6. (Touch the ball of the arrow:) Say it fast. (Slash right, along the arrow:) *rǎ.* Yes, you read the funny word **rǎ.**

ra

Task C Sa [sǎ]

1. Say each sound when I touch it.
- (Point to **s**:) What sound? (Touch under **s**:) *sss.*
- (Point to **a**:) What sound? (Touch under **a**:) *ǎǎǎ.*
2. (Touch the ball of the arrow for **sa**:) Now I'm going to sound out the word. I won't stop between the sounds.
- (Touch under **s, a** as you say:) **sssǎǎǎ.**
3. (Touch the ball of the arrow:) Do it with me. Sound it out. Get ready. (Touch under **s, a**:) *sssǎǎǎ.* (Repeat until the students say the sounds without pausing.)
4. Again. Sound it out. Get ready. (Touch under **s, a**:) *sssǎǎǎ.* (Repeat until firm.)
5. All by yourselves. Sound it out. Get ready. (Touch under **s, a**:) *sssǎǎǎ.* (Repeat until firm.)
6. (Touch the ball of the arrow:) Say it fast. (Slash right, along the arrow:) *sǎ.* Yes, you read the funny word **sǎ.**

sa

Task D At

1. (Point to **a**:) What sound? (Touch under **a**:) *ǎǎǎ.*
2. (Point to **t**:) What sound? (Touch under **t**:) *t.*
3. (Touch the ball of the arrow:) My turn to sound out this word.
- (Touch under **a, t** as you say:) **ǎǎt.** (Do not pause between the sounds.)
4. (Touch the ball of the arrow:) Your turn. Sound it out. Get ready. (Touch under **a, t**:) *ǎǎt.* (Repeat until the students say the sounds without pausing.)

at

To correct:
a. My turn to sound it out. I won't stop between the sounds.
• (Touch under each letter or combination. Say the sounds without pausing between them.)
b. Sound it out with me. Get ready. (Touch under each sound as you and the students say the sounds without pausing between them.)
c. Again. (Repeat step *b* until firm.)
d. (Repeat step 4 until firm.)

5. (Touch the ball of the arrow:) Say it fast. (Slash right, along the arrow:) *At.* Yes, **at.**

at

Task E Ree

1. (Point to **r:**) What sound? (Touch under **r:**) *rrr.*
2. (Point to **ee:**) What sound? (Touch under **ee:**) *ēēē.*
3. (Touch the ball of the arrow:) My turn to sound out this word.
• (Touch under **r, ee** as you say:) **rrrēēē.** (Do not pause between the sounds.)
4. (Touch the ball of the arrow:) Your turn. Sound it out. Get ready. (Touch under **r, ee:**) *rrrēēē.* (Repeat until the students say the sounds without pausing.)
5. (Touch the ball of the arrow:) Say it fast. (Slash right, along the arrow:) *ree.* Yes, **ree.**

ree

Task F Meet

1. (Point to **m:**) What sound? (Touch under **m:**) *mmm.*
2. (Point to **ee:**) What sound? (Touch under **ee:**) *ēēē.*
3. (Point to **t:**) What sound? (Touch under **t:**) *t.*
4. (Touch the ball of the arrow:) My turn to sound out this word.
• (Touch under **m, ee, t** as you say:) **mmmēēēt.** (Do not pause between the sounds.)
5. (Touch the ball of the arrow:) Your turn. Sound it out. Get ready. (Touch under **m, ee, t:**) *mmmēēēt.* (Repeat until the students say the sounds without pausing.)
6. (Touch the ball of the arrow:) Say it fast. (Slash right, along the arrow:) *Meet.* Yes, **meet.**

meet

Task G Me

1. (Point to **m:**) What sound? (Touch under **m:**) *mmm.*
2. (Point to **e:**) What sound? (Touch under **e:**) *ēēē.*
3. (Touch the ball of the arrow:) My turn to sound out this word.
• (Touch under **m, e** as you say:) **mmmēēē.** (Do not pause between the sounds.)
4. (Touch the ball of the arrow:) Your turn. Sound it out. Get ready. (Touch under **m, e:**) *mmmēēē.* (Repeat until the students say the sounds without pausing.)
5. (Touch the ball of the arrow:) Say it fast. (Slash right, along the arrow:) *Me.* Yes, **me.**

me

Task H Ram

1. (Point to **r:**) What sound? (Touch under **r:**) *rrr.*
2. (Point to **a:**) What sound? (Touch under **a:**) *ăăă.*
3. (Point to **m:**) What sound? (Touch under **m:**) *mmm.*
4. (Touch the ball of the arrow:) My turn to sound out this word.
- (Touch under **r, a, m** as you say:) **rrrăăămmm.** (Do not pause between the sounds.)
5. (Touch the ball of the arrow:) Your turn. Sound it out. Get ready. (Touch under **r, a, m:**) *rrrăăămmm.* (Repeat until the students say the sounds without pausing.)
6. (Touch the ball of the arrow:) Say it fast. (Slash right, along the arrow:) *Ram.* Yes, **ram.**

ram

Task I See

1. (Point to **s:**) What sound? (Touch under **s:**) *sss.*
2. (Point to **ee:**) What sound? (Touch under **ee:**) *ēēē.*
3. (Touch the ball of the arrow:) My turn to sound out the word.
- (Touch under **s, ee** as you say:) **sssēēē.** (Do not pause between the sounds.)
4. (Touch the ball of the arrow:) Your turn. Sound it out. Get ready. (Touch under **s, ee:**) *sssēēē.* (Repeat until the students say the sounds without pausing.)
5. (Touch the ball of the arrow:) Say it fast. (Slash right, along the arrow:) *See.* Yes, **see.**

see

Task J Ma [mă]

1. (Point to **m:**) What sound? (Touch under **m:**) *mmm.*
2. (Point to **a:**) What sound? (Touch under **a:**) *ăăă.*
3. (Touch the ball of the arrow:) My turn to sound out this word.
- (Touch under **m, a** as you say:) **mmmăăă.** (Do not pause between the sounds.)
4. (Touch the ball of the arrow:) Your turn. Sound it out. Get ready. (Touch under **m, a:**) *mmmăăă.* (Repeat until the students say the sounds without pausing.)
5. (Touch the ball of the arrow:) Say it fast. (Slash right, along the arrow:) *mă.* Yes, **mă.**

ma

WORKBOOK EXERCISES

Note: Pass out the Workbooks. Direct the students to open their Workbooks to Lesson 3.

- (If the group worked well during the word attack, say:) Everybody, write 6 in Box A at the top of your Workbook lesson. That shows that the group earned 6 points today.
- (If the group did **not** work well during the word attack, say:) You did not earn any group points today, but everybody will get a chance to earn points on the Workbook lesson.
- Now we're going to do exercises in the Workbook. You can earn up to 8 points for these activities.

EXERCISE 6

SOUND DICTATION

1. Everybody, touch part 1 in your Workbook. ✓
• These are the sounds you did before. Say all the sounds once more before you write the letters.
2. Touch the first sound. ✓
• What sound? (Clap.) *d.* Yes, **d.**
3. Touch the next sound. ✓
• What sound? (Clap.) *rrr.* Yes, **rrr.**
4. (Repeat step 3 for each remaining sound.)
5. Now you're going to write the letters for the sounds I say. First sound. (Pause.) **t.** What sound? (Clap.) *t.*
• Write it in the first blank. (Observe students and give feedback.)
6. Next sound. (Pause.) **d.** What sound? (Clap.) *d.*
• Write it in the next blank. (Observe students and give feedback.)

> **To correct *b-d* reversals:**
> Listen. If you can write the letter **C**, you can write the letter for the sound **d**. First you write the letter **C**. Then you make an up-and-down line. (Demonstrate.)

7. (Repeat step 6 for **ăăă, mmm, ēēē, t, sss, d, rrr, mmm, t, ēēē, d, rrr.**)
8. (Check that students can write all the letters without errors.)

EXERCISE 7

NEW SOUND IT OUT: Workbook

1. Everybody, touch part 2. These are some of the words we sounded out earlier. This time, you're going to touch the letters and sound out the words.
2. Touch the ball of the arrow for word 1. ✓
3. Sound it out. Get ready. (Clap for **r, a** as the students touch under **r, a** and say:) *rrrăăă.* (Repeat until the students say the sounds without pausing.)

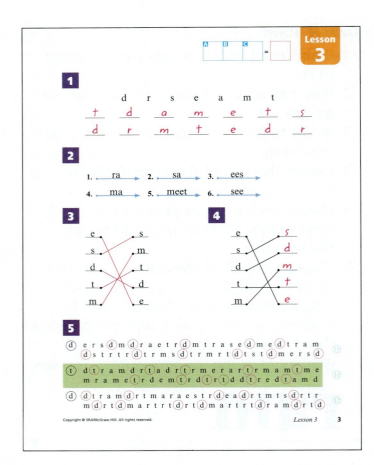

> **To correct:**
> a. My turn to sound it out. I won't stop between the sounds. Touch the letters as I say the sounds. Get ready. (Clap for **r, a** as you say:) **rrrăăă.**
> b. Your turn to sound it out. Get ready. (Clap for **r, a:**) *rrrăăă.*
> c. Again. (Repeat step 3.)

4. Touch the ball of the arrow for word 2. ✓
5. Sound it out. Get ready. (Clap for **s, a** as the students touch under **s, a** and say:) *sssăăă.* (Repeat until the students say the sounds without pausing.)
6. (Repeat steps 4 and 5 for **ees, mă, meet, see.**)

> **Individual test**
> (Call on each student to sound out three words.) Sound out the word. Remember, touch the sounds as you say them. Don't stop between the sounds.

EXERCISE 8
NEW MATCHING SOUNDS

1. Everybody, touch part 3. ✓
• You're going to draw lines to match the letters. Get ready to say the sounds in the first column.
2. Touch the first letter. ✓
• What sound? (Clap.) *ēēē.*
3. Touch the next letter. ✓
• What sound? (Clap.) *sss.*
4. (Repeat step 3 for **d, t, m.**)
5. Later, you'll draw lines to match the letters.

EXERCISE 9
NEW MATCHING AND COPYING SOUNDS

1. Everybody, touch part 4. ✓
2. Later, you'll write letters in the blanks of this matching exercise.

EXERCISE 10
NEW CIRCLE GAME

1. Everybody, touch part 5. ✓
2. What will you circle in the first two lines? (Clap.) *d.*
• How many are there? (Clap.) *11.*
3. What will you circle in the next two lines? (Clap.) *t.*
• How many are there? (Clap.) *11.*
4. What will you circle in the last two lines? (Clap.) *d.*
• How many are there? (Clap.) *12.*
5. Circle the sounds.
6. Now go back and finish parts 3 and 4 in your Workbook. (Observe students and give feedback.)

Note: Record points in Box B for each student's performance on assigned Workbook activities.
0–1 error	8 points
2–3 errors	3 points
4 or more errors	0 points

INDIVIDUAL READING CHECKOUTS

EXERCISE 11
SOUND-IT-OUT CHECKOUT

• Practice sounding out all the words in part 2 without stopping between sounds. You'll each get a turn to sound out all these words. You can earn as many as 6 points for this reading.
• If you sound out all the words with no more than 1 error, you'll earn 6 points.
• If you make more than 1 error, you do not earn any points. But you'll have another chance to earn 6 points by studying the words some more and reading them again.
• (Check the students individually.)
• (Record either 6 or 0 points in Box C.)

Lesson point total

(Tell students to add the points in Boxes A, B, and C and to write this total in the last box at the top of the Workbook page. Maximum for the lesson = 20 points.)

Point Summary Chart

(Tell students to write this point total in the box for Lesson 3 in the Point Summary Chart.)

END OF LESSON 3

Lesson 4

WORD-ATTACK SKILLS

Remember, you can earn 6 points if everybody in the group responds on signal, follows along when somebody else is reading, and tries hard.

━━━━━━ **EXERCISE 1** ━━━━━━

PRONUNCIATIONS: Sounds

> **Note:** Do not write the words on the board. This is an oral exercise.

Task A

1. Listen to the first sound in (pause) **rid.** The first sound is **rrr.** Say it. (Signal.) *rrr.* Yes, **rrr.**
2. (Repeat step 1 until firm.)
3. Listen to the middle sound in (pause) **rid.** The middle sound is **ĭĭĭ.** Say it. (Signal.) *ĭĭĭ.* Yes, **ĭĭĭ.**
4. (Repeat step 3 until firm.)
5. Listen to the last sound in (pause) **rid.** The last sound is **d.** Say it. (Signal.) *d.* Yes, **d.**
6. (Repeat step 5 until firm.)

Task B

1. Listen to the first sound in (pause) **at.** The first sound is **ăăă.** Say it. (Signal.) *ăăă.* Yes, **ăăă.**
2. (Repeat step 1 until firm.)
3. Listen to the last sound in (pause) **at.** The last sound is **t.** Say it. (Signal.) *t.* Yes, **t.**
4. (Repeat step 3 until firm.)

Task C

1. New word. Listen to the first sound in (pause) **seem.** The first sound is **sss.** Say it. (Signal.) *sss.* Yes, **sss.**
2. (Repeat step 1 until firm.)
3. Listen to the middle sound in (pause) **seem.** The middle sound is **ēēē.** Say it. (Signal.) *ēēē.* Yes, **ēēē.**
4. (Repeat step 3 until firm.)
5. Listen to the last sound in (pause) **seem.** The last sound is **mmm.** Say it. (Signal.) *mmm.* Yes, **mmm.**
6. (Repeat step 5 until firm.)

Task D

1. Let's do those sounds again the fast way. Listen: **rrr.** Say it. (Signal.) *rrr.*
2. Listen: **ēēē.** Say it. (Signal.) *ēēē.*
3. Listen: **t.** Say it. (Signal.) *t.*
4. Listen: **sss.** Say it. (Signal.) *sss.*
5. Listen: **ĭĭĭ.** Say it. (Signal.) *ĭĭĭ.*
6. Listen: **mmm.** Say it. (Signal.) *mmm.*
7. Listen: **d.** Say it. (Signal.) *d.*
8. Listen: **ăăă.** Say it. (Signal.) *ăăă.*

> **Individual test**
> (Call on different students to say two sounds. Do not present the same two sounds to each student.)

━━━━━━ **EXERCISE 2** ━━━━━━

PRONUNCIATIONS

> **Note:** Do not write the words on the board. This is an oral exercise.

Task A

1. Listen. She was **mad.** (Pause.) **Mad.** Say it. (Signal.) *Mad.*
2. Next word. Listen. They wrestled on a **mat.** (Pause.) **Mat.** Say it. (Signal.) *Mat.*
3. Next word: **ram.** Say it. (Signal.) *Ram.*
4. (Repeat step 3 for **sat, reem, seem.**)
5. (Repeat all the words until firm.)

NEW Task B Sit, rim, fin

1. I'll say words that have the sound **ĭĭĭ.** What sound? (Signal.) *ĭĭĭ.* **Yes, ĭĭĭ.**
2. (Repeat step 1 until firm.)
3. Listen: **sit, rim, fin.** Your turn: **sit.** Say it. (Signal.) *Sit.* Yes, **sit.**
4. Next word: **rim.** Say it. (Signal.) *Rim.* Yes, **rim.**
5. Next word: **fin.** Say it. (Signal.) *Fin.* Yes, **fin.**
6. (Repeat steps 3–5 until firm.)
7. What's the middle sound in the word **rrrĭĭĭmmm?** (Signal.) *ĭĭĭ.* Yes, **ĭĭĭ.**
8. (Repeat step 7 until firm.)

EXERCISE 3
NEW SAY THE SOUNDS

> **Note:** Do not write the words on the board. This is an oral exercise.

1. First you're going to say a word slowly without stopping between the sounds. Then you're going to say the word fast.
2. Listen: **sssēēē.** (Hold up a finger for each sound.)
3. Say the sounds in (pause) **sssēēē.** Get ready. (Hold up a finger for each sound.) *sssēēē.* (Repeat until the students say the sounds without stopping.)
4. Say it fast. (Signal.) *See.*
5. What word? (Signal.) *See.* Yes, **see.**
6. (Repeat steps 2–5 for **sad, mad, mat, me, seed, in, if, sat, ran, rat.**)

EXERCISE 4
SOUND INTRODUCTION

1. (Point to **i:**) One sound this letter makes is ĭĭĭ. What sound? (Touch.) *ĭĭĭ.*
2. (Point to **d:**) This letter makes the sound **d.** What sound? (Touch.) *d.*
3. Say each sound when I touch it.
4. (Point to **i:**) What sound? (Touch under **i:**) *ĭĭĭ.*
5. (Repeat step 4 for **d, ē, d, r, t, s, ă, m.**)

> **To correct:**
> a. (Say the sound loudly as soon as you hear an error.)
> b. (Point to the sound:) This sound is _____. What sound? (Touch.)
> c. (Repeat the series of letters until all the students can correctly identify all the sounds in order.)

6. (Point to the circled letters:) The sound for one of these letters is the same as the letter name. That's the name you say when you say the alphabet.

7. (Point to **i:**) Listen: ĭĭĭ. Is that a letter name? (Signal.) *No.* Right, it isn't.
8. (Point to **a:**) Listen: ăăă. Is that a letter name? (Signal.) *No.* Right, it isn't.
9. (Point to **e:**) Listen: ēēē. Is that a letter name? (Signal.) *Yes.*
   Yes, it is. Remember, the sound you're learning for ēēē is the same as the letter name.

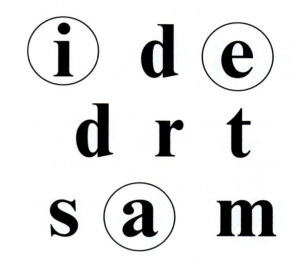

> **Individual test**
> I'll call on different students to say all the sounds. If everybody I call on can say all the sounds without making a mistake, we'll go on to the next exercise. (Call on two or three students. Touch under each sound. Each student says all the sounds.)

—————— **EXERCISE 5** ——————
NEW **WORD READING**

Task A Ees

1. You're going to read each word. First you sound it out; then you say it fast.
2. (Touch the ball of the arrow for the first word:) Sound it out. Get ready. (Touch under **ee, s:**) ēēēsss. (Repeat until the students say the sounds without pausing.)

ees

> **To correct sound errors:**
> a. (Say the correct sound loudly as soon as you hear an error.)
> b. (Point to the sound:) What sound? (Touch.)
> c. (Repeat until firm.)
> d. (Repeat step 2.)

3. Again. Sound it out. Get ready. (Touch under **ee, s:**) ēēēsss. (Repeat until firm.)
4. (Touch the ball of the arrow:) Say it fast. (Slash right, along the arrow:) ees. Yes, **ees**.

> **To correct say-it-fast errors:**
> a. (Say the correct word:) **ees**.
> b. (Touch the ball of the arrow:) Say it fast. (Slash right:) ees.
> c. (Return to step 2.)

ees

Task B Eem

1. (Touch the ball of the arrow:) Sound it out. Get ready. (Touch under **ee, m:**) ēēēmmm. (Repeat until the students say the sounds without pausing.)
2. Again. Sound it out. Get ready. (Touch under **ee, m:**) ēēēmmm. (Repeat until firm.)
3. (Touch the ball of the arrow:) Say it fast. (Slash right:) eem. Yes, **eem**.

eem

Task C Eet

1. (Touch the ball of the arrow:) Sound it out. Get ready. (Touch under **ee, t:**) ēēēt. (Repeat until the students say the sounds without pausing.)
2. Again. Sound it out. Get ready. (Touch under **ee, t:**) ēēēt. (Repeat until firm.)
3. (Touch the ball of the arrow:) Say it fast. (Slash right:) eet. Yes, **eet**.

eet

Task D At

1. (Touch the ball of the arrow:) Sound it out. Get ready. (Touch under **a, t:**) ăăăt. (Repeat until the students say the sounds without pausing.)
2. Again. Sound it out. Get ready. (Touch under **a, t:**) ăăăt. (Repeat until firm.)
3. (Touch the ball of the arrow:) Say it fast. (Slash right:) At. Yes, **at**.

at

Task E Am

1. (Touch the ball of the arrow:) Sound it out. Get ready. (Touch under **a, m**:) *ăăămmm.* (Repeat until the students say the sounds without pausing.)
2. Again. Sound it out. Get ready. (Touch under **a, m**:) *ăăămmm.* (Repeat until firm.)
3. (Touch the ball of the arrow:) Say it fast. (Slash right:) *Am.* Yes, **am.**

am

Task F Me

1. (Touch the ball of the arrow:) Sound it out. Get ready. (Touch under **m, e**:) *mmmēēē.* (Repeat until the students say the sounds without pausing.)
2. Again. Sound it out. Get ready. (Touch under **m, e**:) *mmmēēē.* (Repeat until firm.)
3. (Touch the ball of the arrow:) Say it fast. (Slash right:) *Me.* Yes, **me.**

me

Task G Ma [mă]

1. (Touch the ball of the arrow:) Sound it out. Get ready. (Touch under **m, a**:) *mmmăăă.* (Repeat until the students say the sounds without pausing.)
2. Again. Sound it out. Get ready. (Touch under **m, a**:) *mmmăăă.* (Repeat until firm.)
3. (Touch the ball of the arrow:) Say it fast. (Slash right:) *mă.* Yes, **mă.**

ma

Task H See

1. (Touch the ball of the arrow:) Sound it out. Get ready. (Touch under **s, ee**:) *sssēēē.* (Repeat until the students say the sounds without pausing.)
2. Again. Sound it out. Get ready. (Touch under **s, ee**:) *sssēēē.* (Repeat until firm.)
3. (Touch the ball of the arrow:) Say it fast. (Slash right:) *See.* Yes, **see.**

see

Task I Sa [să]

1. (Touch the ball of the arrow:) Sound it out. Get ready. (Touch under **s, a**:) *sssăăă.* (Repeat until the students say the sounds without pausing.)
2. Again. Sound it out. Get ready. (Touch under **s, a**:) *sssăăă.* (Repeat until firm.)
3. (Touch the ball of the arrow:) Say it fast. (Slash right:) *să.* Yes, **să.**

sa

━━━━━ **EXERCISE 6** ━━━━━

WORD READING

Task A Sat

1. Say each sound when I touch it.
- (Point to **s:**) What sound? (Touch under **s:**) *sss.*
- (Point to **a:**) What sound? (Touch under **a:**) *ăăă.*
- (Point to **t:**) What sound? (Touch under **t:**) *t.*
2. (Touch the ball of the arrow for **sat:**) Now I'm going to sound out the word. I won't stop between the sounds.
- (Touch under **s, a, t:**) *sssăăăt.*
3. (Touch the ball of the arrow:) Do it with me. Sound it out. Get ready. (Touch under **s, a, t:**) *sssăăăt.* (Repeat until the students say the sounds without pausing.)
4. Again. Sound it out. Get ready. (Touch under **s, a, t:**) *sssăăăt.* (Repeat until firm.)
5. All by yourselves. Sound it out. Get ready. (Touch under **s, a, t:**) *sssăăăt.* (Repeat until firm.)
6. (Touch the ball of the arrow:) Say it fast. (Slash right, along the arrow:) *Sat.* Yes, you read the word **sat.**

sat

Task B Sad

1. Say each sound when I touch it.
- (Point to **s:**) What sound? (Touch under **s:**) *sss.*
- (Point to **a:**) What sound? (Touch under **a:**) *ăăă.*
- (Point to **d:**) What sound? (Touch under **d:**) *d.*
2. (Touch the ball of the arrow for **sad:**) Now I'm going to sound out the word. I won't stop between sounds.
- (Touch under **s, a, d** as you say:) *sssăăăd.*

3. (Touch the ball of the arrow:) Do it with me. Sound it out. Get ready. (Touch under **s, a, d:**) *sssăăăd.* (Repeat until the students say the sounds without pausing.)
4. Again. Sound it out. Get ready. (Touch under **s, a, d:**) *sssăăăd.* (Repeat until firm.)
5. All by yourselves. Sound it out. Get ready. (Touch under **s, a, d:**) *sssăăăd.* (Repeat until firm.)
6. (Touch the ball of the arrow:) Say it fast. (Slash right, along the arrow:) *Sad.* Yes, you read the word **sad.**

sad

━━━━━ **EXERCISE 7** ━━━━━

NEW PRONUNCIATIONS

1. Listen. We planted a **seed.** (Pause.) **Seed.** Say it. (Signal.) *Seed.*
2. I'll say the first sound in the word **ssseeed.** (Pause.) **sss.** What's the first sound? (Signal.) *sss.* Yes, **sss.**
3. Say the middle sound in the word **ssseeed.** Get ready. (Signal.) *ēēē.* Yes, *ēēē.*

> **To correct:**
>   a. (Hold up one finger.) **sss.**
>   b. (Hold up two fingers.) **ēēē.**
>   c. What's the middle sound in **ssseeed?** (Signal.) *ēēē.* Yes, *ēēē.*
>   d. (Repeat step 3 until firm.)

4. Listen: **sad.** Say it. (Signal.) *Sad.*
5. I'll say the first sound in the word **sssăăăd.** (Pause.) **sss.** What's the first sound? (Signal.) *sss.* Yes, **sss.**
6. Say the middle sound in the word **sssăăăd.** Get ready. (Signal.) *ăăă.* Yes, *ăăă.*
7. One of those words has the middle sound *ēēē.* I'll say both words again: **seed** (pause) **sad.** Which word has the middle sound *ēēē?* (Signal.) *Seed.* Yes, **seed.**

WORKBOOK EXERCISES

Note: Pass out the Workbooks. Direct the students to open their Workbooks to Lesson 4.

- (If the group worked well during the word attack, say:) Everybody, write 6 in Box A at the top of your Workbook lesson. That shows that the group earned 6 points today.
- (If the group did **not** work well during the word attack, say:) You did not earn any group points today, but everybody will get a chance to earn points on the Workbook lesson.
- Now we're going to do exercises in the Workbook. You can earn up to 8 points for these activities.

EXERCISE 8

SOUND DICTATION

1. Everybody, touch part 1 in your Workbook. ✓
- These are the sounds you did before. Say all the sounds once more before you write the letters.
2. Touch the first sound. ✓
- What sound? (Clap.) ĭĭĭ. Yes, ĭĭĭ.
3. Touch the next sound. ✓
- What sound? (Clap.) t. Yes, t.
4. (Repeat step 3 for each remaining sound.)

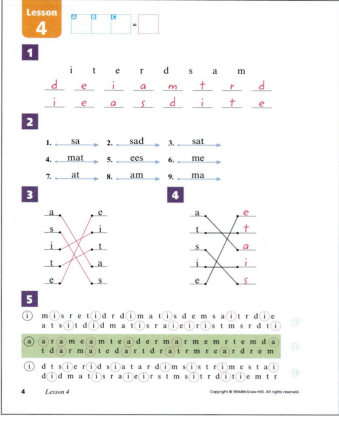

5. Now you're going to write the letters for the sounds I say. First sound. (Pause.) **d.** What sound? (Clap.) *d.*
- Write it in the first blank. (Observe students and give feedback.)

> **To correct b-d reversals:**
> Listen. If you can write the letter **C,** you can write the letter for the sound **d.** First you write the letter **C.** Then you make an up-and-down line. (Demonstrate.)

6. Next sound. (Pause.) **ēēē.** What sound? (Clap.) *ēēē.*
- Write it in the next blank. (Observe students and give feedback.)
7. (Repeat step 6 for ĭĭĭ, ăăă, mmm, t, rrr, d, ĭĭĭ, ēēē, ăăă, sss, d, ĭĭĭ, t, ēēē.)
8. (Check that students can write all the letters without errors.)

EXERCISE 9
SOUND IT OUT: Workbook

1. Everybody, touch part 2. ✓
• These are some of the words we sounded out earlier. This time, you're going to touch the letters and sound out the words.
2. Touch the ball of the arrow for word 1. ✓
3. Sound it out. Get ready. (Clap for **s, a** as the students touch under **s, a** and say:) *ssssăăă.* (Repeat until the students say the sounds without pausing.)

> **To correct:**
> a. My turn to sound it out. I won't stop between the sounds. Touch the letters as I say the sounds. Get ready. (Clap for **s, a** as you say:) **sssăăă.**
> b. Your turn to sound it out. Get ready. (Clap for **s, a:**) *sssăăă.*
> c. Again. (Repeat step 3.)

4. Touch the ball of the arrow for word 2. ✓
5. Sound it out. Get ready. (Clap for **s, a, d** as the students touch under **s, a, d** and say:) *sssăăăd.* (Repeat until the students say the sounds without pausing.)
6. (Repeat steps 4 and 5 for **sat, mat, ees, me, at, am, ma.**)

> **Individual test**
> (Call on each student to sound out three words.) Sound out the word. Remember, touch the sounds as you say them. Don't stop between the sounds.

EXERCISE 10
MATCHING SOUNDS

1. Everybody, touch part 3. ✓
• Get ready to say the sounds in the first column.
2. Touch the first letter. ✓
• What sound? (Clap.) *ăăă.*
3. Touch the next letter. ✓
• What sound? (Clap.) *sss.*

4. (Repeat step 3 for ĭ, t, ē.)
5. Later, you'll draw lines to match the letters.

EXERCISE 11
MATCHING AND COPYING SOUNDS

1. Everybody, touch part 4. ✓
2. Later, you'll write letters in the blanks of this matching exercise.

EXERCISE 12
CIRCLE GAME

1. Everybody, touch part 5. ✓
2. What will you circle in the first two lines? (Clap.) *ĭĭĭ.*
• How many are there? (Clap.) *13.*
3. What will you circle in the next two lines? (Clap.) *ăăă.*
• How many are there? (Clap.) *11.*
4. What will you circle in the last two lines? (Clap.) *ĭĭĭ.*
• How many are there? (Clap.) *14.*
5. Circle the sounds and finish parts 3 and 4 in your Workbook.
(Observe students and give feedback.)

EXERCISE 13
NEW WORKBOOK CHECK

> **Note:** See the Teacher's Guide for Workbook correction procedures.

1. (Check each student's Workbook.)
2. (Award points for Workbook performance.)
3. (Record the student's total points in Box B.)

0–1 error	8 points
2–3 errors	3 points
4 or more errors	0 points

INDIVIDUAL READING CHECKOUTS

━━━━━━ **EXERCISE 14** ━━━━━━
SOUND-IT-OUT CHECKOUT

- Practice sounding out all the words in part 2 without stopping between sounds. You'll each get a turn to sound out all these words. You can earn as many as 6 points for this reading.
- If you sound out all the words with no more than 1 error, you'll earn 6 points.
- If you make more than 1 error, you do not earn any points. But you'll have another chance to earn 6 points by studying the words some more and reading them again.
- (Check the students individually.)
- (Record either 6 or 0 points in Box C.)

Lesson point total

(Tell students to add the points in Boxes A, B, and C and to write this total in the last box at the top of the Workbook page. Maximum for the lesson = 20 points.)

Point Summary Chart

(Tell students to write this point total in the box for Lesson 4 in the Point Summary Chart.)

END OF LESSON 4

MASTERY TEST 1
— AFTER LESSON 4, BEFORE LESSON 5 —

> **Note:** Test each student individually. Record performance for each student on the *Decoding A* Mastery Test Student Profile. Reproducible Student Profile forms are at the back of the Teacher's Guide. Administer the test so that other students do not overhear the student being tested.

me

sat

ram

Part A Pronunciation (Phonemic Awareness)

1. You're going to say words that have the sound ĭĭĭ. What sound? ĭĭĭ.
2. (Test item.) Listen: **fin.** Say it. *Fin.*
3. (Test item.) Next word: **sit.** Say it. *Sit.*
4. (Test item.) Next word: **rim.** Say it. *Rim.*

Part B Word reading (Phonics)

1. You're going to read each word. First you sound it out; then you say it fast.
2. (Touch the ball of the arrow for **me:**) Sound it out. (Touch under **m, e:**) *mmmēēē.* (The student should not pause between sounds.)
3. (Test item.) Again. Sound it out. (Touch under **m, e:**) *mmmēēē.* (The student should not pause between sounds.)
4. (Test item. Touch the ball of the arrow for **me:**) Say it fast. (Slash right:) *Me.*
5. (Repeat steps 2–4 for **sat [sssăăăt], ram [rrrăăămmm].**)

Scoring the test

1. (Count each student's errors on the test. Write these numbers in the Test 1 boxes on the *Decoding A* Mastery Test Student Profile form. Circle **P** or **F.**)
2. (When all students have been tested, record each student's **P** or **F** score on the *Decoding A* Mastery Test Group Summary form under Test 1. Reproducible summary forms are at the back of the Teacher's Guide.)
- (Pass criterion: 0 errors. Circle **P.**)
- (Fail criterion: 1 or more errors. Circle **F.**)

Remedies

(If more than 25 percent of the students missed any words in Pronunciation or Word reading, repeat Lessons 3 and 4. Permission is granted to reproduce the Workbook pages for these lessons for classroom use. Then retest.)

WORD-ATTACK SKILLS

Remember, you can earn 6 points if everybody in the group responds on signal, follows along when somebody else is reading, and tries hard.

━━━━━━ **EXERCISE 1** ━━━━━━

PRONUNCIATIONS: Sounds

> **Note:** Do not write the words on the board. This is an oral exercise.

Task A

1. Listen to the first sound in (pause) **ask.** The first sound is **ăăă.** Say it. (Signal.) *ăăă.* Yes, **ăăă.**
2. (Repeat step 1 until firm.)
3. Listen to the middle sound in (pause) **ask.** The middle sound is **sss.** Say it. (Signal.) *sss.* Yes, **sss.**
4. (Repeat step 3 until firm.)
5. Listen to the last sound in (pause) **ask.** The last sound is **k.** Say it. (Signal.) *k.* Yes, **k.**
6. (Repeat step 5 until firm.)

Task B

1. Listen to the first sound in (pause) **heat.** The first sound is **h.** Say it. (Signal.) *h.* Yes, **h.**
2. (Repeat step 1 until firm.)
3. Listen to the middle sound in (pause) **heat.** The middle sound is **ēēē.** Say it. (Signal.) *ēēē.* Yes, **ēēē.**
4. (Repeat step 3 until firm.)
5. Listen to the last sound in (pause) **heat.** The last sound is **t.** Say it. (Signal.) *t.* Yes, **t.**
6. (Repeat step 5 until firm.)

Task C

1. New word. Listen to the first sound in (pause) **rat.** The first sound is **rrr.** Say it. (Signal.) *rrr.* Yes, **rrr.**
2. (Repeat step 1 until firm.)
3. Listen to the middle sound in (pause) **rat.** The middle sound is **ăăă.** Say it. (Signal.) *ăăă.* Yes, **ăăă.**

4. (Repeat step 3 until firm.)
5. Listen to the last sound in (pause) **rat.** The last sound is **t.** Say it. (Signal.) *t.* Yes, **t.**
6. (Repeat step 5 until firm.)

Task D

1. Let's do those sounds again the fast way. Listen: **h.** Say it. (Signal.) *h.*
2. Listen: **ăăă.** Say it. (Signal.) *ăăă.*
3. Listen: **t.** Say it. (Signal.) *t.*
4. Listen: **sss.** Say it. (Signal.) *sss.*
5. Listen: **k.** Say it. (Signal.) *k.*
6. Listen: **ēēē.** Say it. (Signal.) *ēēē.*
7. Listen: **rrr.** Say it. (Signal.) *rrr.*

> **Individual test**
> (Call on different students to say two sounds. Do not present the same two sounds to each student.)

━━━━━━ **EXERCISE 2** ━━━━━━

PRONUNCIATIONS

> **Note:** Do not write the words on the board. This is an oral exercise.

Task A

1. Listen. Her pants did not **fit.** (Pause.) **Fit.** Say it. (Signal.) *Fit.*
2. Next word: **fa.** Say it. (Signal.) *fa.*
3. (Repeat step 2 for **see, fish, fat.**)
4. (Repeat all the words until firm.)

Task B Hit, fill, him

1. I'll say words that have the sound **ĭĭĭ.** What sound? (Signal.) *ĭĭĭ.* Yes, **ĭĭĭ.**
2. (Repeat step 1 until firm.)
3. Listen: **hit, fill, him.** Your turn: **hit.** Say it. (Signal.) *Hit.* Yes, **hit.**
4. Next word: **fill.** Say it. (Signal.) *Fill.* Yes, **fill.**
5. Next word: **him.** Say it. (Signal.) *Him.* Yes, **him.**
6. (Repeat steps 3–5 until firm.)
7. What's the middle sound in the word **fffĭĭĭlll?** (Signal.) *ĭĭĭ.* Yes, **ĭĭĭ.**
8. (Repeat step 7 until firm.)

NEW *Task C* **Sack, seek**

1. Listen: **sack.** Say it. (Signal.) *Sack.*
2. I'll say the first sound in the word **sssăăăck.** (Pause.) **sss.** What's the first sound? (Signal.) *sss.* Yes, **sss.**
3. Say the middle sound in the word **sssăăăck.** Get ready. (Signal.) *ăăă.* Yes, **ăăă.**

> To correct:
> a. (Hold up one finger.) **sss.**
> b. (Hold up two fingers.) **ăăă.**
> c. What's the middle sound in **sssăăăck?** (Signal.) *ăăă.* Yes, **ăăă.**
> d. (Repeat step 3 until firm.)

4. Listen: **seek.** Say it. (Signal.) *Seek.*
5. I'll say the first sound in the word **sssēēēk.** (Pause.) **sss.** What's the first sound? (Signal.) *sss.* Yes, **sss.**
6. Say the middle sound in the word **sssēēēk.** Get ready. (Signal.) *ēēē.* Yes, **ēēē.**
7. One of those words has the middle sound **ēēē.** I'll say both words again: **sack** (pause) **seek.** Which word has the middle sound **ēēē?** (Signal.) *Seek.* Yes, **seek.**

EXERCISE 3
SAY THE SOUNDS

> **Note:** Do not write the words on the board. This is an oral exercise.

1. First you're going to say a word slowly without stopping between the sounds. Then you're going to say the word fast.
2. Listen: **sssēēēt.** (Hold up a finger for each sound.)
3. Say the sounds in (pause) **sssēēēt.** Get ready. (Hold up a finger for each sound.) *sssēēēt.* (Repeat until the students say the sounds without stopping.)
4. Say it fast. (Signal.) *Seat.*
5. What word? (Signal.) *Seat.* Yes, **seat.**
6. (Repeat steps 2–5 for **sat, sit, eat, at, it, ran, fish, am, rim.**)

EXERCISE 4
SOUND INTRODUCTION

1. (Point to **i:**) One sound this letter makes is **ĭĭĭ.** What sound? (Touch.) *ĭĭĭ.*
2. Your turn. Say each sound when I touch it.
3. (Point to **i:**) What sound? (Touch under **i:**) *ĭĭĭ.*
4. (Repeat step 3 for **r, ă, ē, m, ĭ, d, ă, s.**)

> To correct:
> a. (Say the sound loudly as soon as you hear an error.)
> b. (Point to the sound:) This sound is _____. What sound? (Touch.)
> c. (Repeat the series of letters until all the students can correctly identify all the sounds in order.)

i r a
e m i
d a s

> **Individual test**
> I'll call on different students to say all the sounds. If everybody I call on can say all the sounds without making a mistake, we'll go on to the next exercise. (Call on two or three students. Touch under each sound. Each student says all the sounds.)

Task E Ron, ran

1. Listen: **ron** (pause) **ran.** Say those words. (Signal.) *Ron, ran.* (Repeat until firm.)
2. One of those words has the middle sound **ŏŏŏ.** I'll say the words again: **ron** (pause) **ran.** Which word has the middle sound **ŏŏŏ?** (Signal.) *Ron.* Yes, **ron.**
3. Which word has the middle sound **ăăă?** (Signal.) *Ran.* Yes, **ran.**

EXERCISE 3
WORD READING

Task A

1. Read these words.
2. (Touch the ball of the arrow for **cats:**) Sound it out. Get ready. (Touch under **c, a, t, s:**) *căăătsss.* (Repeat until the students say the sounds without pausing.)
3. Again. Sound it out. Get ready. (Touch under **c, a, t, s:**) *căăătsss.* (Repeat until firm.)
4. (Touch the ball of the arrow:) Say it fast. (Slash right:) *Cats.* Yes, **cats.**
5. (Touch the ball of the arrow for **cash:**) Sound it out. Get ready. (Touch under c, a, sh:) *căăăshshsh.* (Repeat until the students say the sounds without pausing.)
6. Again. Sound it out. Get ready. (Touch under **c, a, sh:**) *căăăshshsh.* (Repeat until firm.)
7. (Touch the ball of the arrow:) Say it fast. (Slash right:) *Cash.* Yes, **cash.**
8. (Repeat steps 5–7 for **cast, math, hot, seems, on, teeth, in, dish, dash, shad, con.**)

cats ●————————————————→

cash ●————————————————→

cast ●————————————————→

math ●————————————————→

hot ●————————————————→

seems ●————————————————→

on ●————————————————→

teeth ●————————————————→

in ●————————————————→

dish ●————————————————→

dash ●————————————————→

shad ●————————————————→

con ●————————————————→

9. (Touch the ball of the arrow for **can:**) Sound it out. Get ready. (Touch under **c, a, n:**) *căăănnn.* (Repeat until the students say the sounds without pausing.)
10. Again. Sound it out. Get ready. (Touch under **c, a, n:**) *căăănnn.* (Repeat until firm.)
11. (Touch the ball of the arrow:) Say it fast. (Slash right:) *Can.* Yes, **can.**
12. (Repeat steps 9–11 for **rid, rod, see, she.**)

Task B **Word reading the fast way**

1. You're going to read these words the fast way.
2. (Touch the ball of the arrow for **hot.** Pause 4 seconds.) What word? (Slash right:) *Hot.*
3. (Touch the ball for **is.** Pause 4 seconds.) What word? (Slash right:) *Is.*
4. (Repeat step 3 for **his, seems, see, she.**)

can

rid

rod

see

she

hot

is

his

seems

see

she

WORKBOOK EXERCISES

> **Note:** Pass out the Workbooks. Direct the students to open to Lesson 21.

(Award 6 points if the group worked well during the word attack. Remind the students of the points they can earn in their Workbook.)

EXERCISE 4

SOUND DICTATION

1. I'll say the sounds. You write the letters in part 1 in your Workbook.
2. First sound. (Pause.) **d.** What sound? (Signal.) *d.*
   - Write it in the first blank.
     (Observe students and give feedback.)
3. Next sound. (Pause.) **k.** What sound? (Signal.) *k.*
   - Write it.
     (Observe students and give feedback.)
4. (Repeat step 3 for **ŏŏŏ, ĭĭĭ, h, nnn, thththth, ăăă, ēēē, shshsh, sss, mmm.**)
5. (Repeat sounds students had trouble with.)

EXERCISE 5

NEW **WORD COMPLETION**

1. Everybody, touch the first arrow in part 2 in your Workbook. ✓
2. You're going to write the word (pause) **it** on the first arrow. What word? (Signal.) *It.* Yes, **it.**
   - Write (pause) **it** on the first arrow.
     (Observe students and give feedback.)
3. Now you're going to change (pause) **it** to say (pause) **sit.**
   - Listen: **sit.** What is the first sound in (pause) **sit?** (Signal.) *sss.* Yes, **sss.**
   - Fix it up to say **sit.**
     (Observe students and give feedback.)

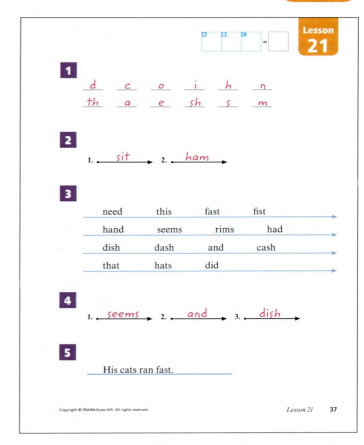

4. Listen. You started with a word. What word? (Signal.) *It.* Yes, **it.**
   - What word do you have now? (Signal.) *Sit.* Yes, **sit.**
5. Touch the next arrow. ✓
   - You're going to write the word (pause) **am.** What word? (Signal.) *Am.* Yes, **am.**
   - Write (pause) **am** on the arrow.
     (Observe students and give feedback.)
6. Now you're going to change (pause) **am** to say (pause) **ham.**
   - Listen: **ham.** What is the first sound in (pause) **ham?** (Signal.) *h.* Yes, **h.**
   - Fix it up to say **ham.**
     (Observe students and give feedback.)
7. Listen. You started with a word. What word? (Signal.) *Am.* Yes, **am.**
   - What word do you have now? (Signal.) *Ham.* Yes, **ham.**

EXERCISE 6

READING THE FAST WAY: Workbook

1. Touch part 3 in your Workbook. ✓
• There are a lot of words on the top line. You're going to read them the fast way.
2. First word. (Pause.) What word? (Signal.) *Need.*
3. Next word. (Pause.) What word? (Signal.) *This.*
4. (Repeat step 3 for **fast, fist**.)
5. (Repeat steps 2–4 until the students can correctly identify all the words on the line in order.)
6. (Repeat steps 2–5 for each remaining line: **hand, seems, rims, had; dish, dash, and, cash; that, hats, did**.)

> **Individual test**
> Practice saying the words to yourself. In a minute, I'll give everybody a turn to read several words the fast way. (Call on each student to read a line of words.)

EXERCISE 7

WORD COPYING

1. Everybody, touch part 4 in your Workbook. ✓
• You're going to write some of the words you just read.
2. The word you're going to write on the first arrow is **seems**. What word? (Signal.) *Seems.*
3. Find **seems** and write it just as it is written in part 3.
(Observe students and give feedback.)
4. The word you're going to write on the next arrow is **and**. What word? (Signal.) *And.*
5. Find **and** and write it just as it is written in part 3.
(Observe students and give feedback.)
6. (Repeat steps 4 and 5 for **dish**.)

EXERCISE 8

SENTENCE READING

Task A

1. Everybody, touch part 5. ✓
• You're going to read each word in the sentence the fast way.
2. Touch under the first word. ✓
• What word? (Signal.) *His.*
3. Next word. (Students touch under the next word.) ✓
• What word? (Signal.) *Cats.*
4. (Repeat step 3 for **ran, fast**.)
5. (Repeat steps 2–4 until the students correctly identify all the words in the sentence in order.)

> **Individual test**
> Everybody, point to the first word in the sentence. (Call on a student.) Take your time. See if you can read all the words in this sentence the fast way without making a mistake. Everybody else, touch under the words that are read. (Call on different students to read the sentence.)

Task B

1. Everybody, touch the first word of the sentence. ✓
2. I'll read the sentence. Follow along. **His cats ran fast.**
3. Here are some questions:
   a. Everybody, how did his cats run? (Signal.) *Fast.*
   b. Did he have one cat or more than one? (Signal.) *More than one.*

EXERCISE 9

WORD COMPLETION

1. Everybody, touch part 6. ✓
2. Sound out the word on the first arrow.
   Get ready. (Clap for **s, ee:**) *sssēēē.*
   - What word? (Signal.) *See.* Yes, **see.**
3. Fix it up to say (pause) **seed.** (Pause.)
   Seed. What word? (Signal.) *Seed.*
   Yes, **seed.**
   - Fix it up.
     (Observe students and give feedback.)
4. Sound out the word on the next arrow.
   Get ready. (Clap for **th, a:**) *thththăăă.*
   - What word? (Signal.) *tha.* Yes, **tha.**
5. Fix it up to say (pause) **that.** (Pause.) **That.**
   What word? (Signal.) *That.* Yes, **that.**
   - Fix it up.
     (Observe students and give feedback.)
6. Sound out the word on the next arrow.
   Get ready. (Clap for **f, i:**) *fffĭĭĭ.*
   - What word? (Signal.) *fi.* Yes, **fi.**
7. Fix it up to say (pause) **fit.** (Pause.) **Fit.**
   What word? (Signal.) *Fit.* Yes, **fit.**
   - Fix it up.
     (Observe students and give feedback.)
8. Sound out the word on the next arrow.
   Get ready. (Clap for **f, i:**) *fffĭĭĭ.*
   - What word? (Signal.) *fi.* Yes, **fi.**
9. Fix it up to say (pause) **fin.** (Pause.) **Fin.**
   What word? (Signal.) *Fin.* Yes, **fin.**
   - Fix it up.
     (Observe students and give feedback.)

> **Individual test**
> I'll call on different students to read words in part 6. First word. (Call on a student.) What word? (Call on different students to read the remaining words.)

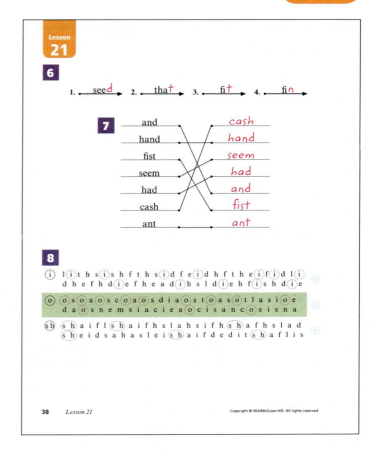

EXERCISE 10

MATCHING COMPLETION

1. Everybody, touch part 7. ✓
   - Read the words the fast way.
2. Touch under the first word. ✓
   - What word? (Signal.) *And.*
3. Next word. ✓
   - What word? (Signal.) *Hand.*
4. (Repeat step 3 for **fist, seem, had, cash, ant.**)
5. Later, you're going to write the words in the second column.

EXERCISE 11

CIRCLE GAME

1. Everybody, touch part 8. ✓
2. What will you circle in the first two lines? (Signal.) *ĭĭĭ.*
3. What will you circle in the next two lines? (Signal.) *ŏŏŏ.*
4. What will you circle in the last two lines? (Signal.) *shshsh.*
5. Circle the sounds and finish the rest of your Workbook lesson.

EXERCISE 12

NEW WORKBOOK CHECK

1. (Check each student's Workbook.)
2. (Award points for Workbook performance.)
3. (Record the student's total points in Box B.)

0–2 errors	8 points
3–4 errors	4 points
5–6 errors	2 points
7 or more errors	0 points

INDIVIDUAL READING CHECKOUTS

EXERCISE 13

WORD-READING CHECKOUT

- Study the words in your Workbook. You'll each get a turn to read all these words the fast way. You can earn as many as 6 points for this reading.
- If you read all the words with no more than 1 error, you'll earn 6 points.
- If you make more than 1 error, you do not earn any points. But you'll have another chance to earn 6 points by studying the words some more and reading them again.
- (Check the students individually.)
- (Record either 6 or 0 points in Box C.)

Lesson point total

(Tell students to write the point total in the last box at the top of the Workbook page. Maximum for the lesson = 20 points.)

Point Summary Chart

(Tell students to write this point total in the box for Lesson 21 in the Point Summary Chart.)

END OF LESSON 21

WORD-ATTACK SKILLS

EXERCISE 1
SOUND INTRODUCTION

1. (Point to **ing**:) These letters usually make the sound **ing**. What sound? (Touch.) *ing*.
2. (Point to **g**:) This letter usually make the sound **g**. What sound? (Touch.) *g*.
3. Say each sound when I touch it.
4. (Point to **ing**:) What sound? (Touch.) *ing*. Yes, **ing**.
5. (Repeat step 4 for **g, m, n, th, g, sh, ŏ, ē, ĭ ă, ing**.)

$$\text{ing} \quad \text{g}$$
$$\text{m} \quad \text{n} \quad \text{th}$$
$$\text{g} \quad \text{sh}$$
$$\text{o} \quad \text{e} \quad \text{i}$$
$$\text{a} \quad \text{ing}$$

> **Individual test**
> I'll call on different students to say all the sounds. If everybody I call on can say all the sounds without making a mistake, we'll go on to the next exercise. (Call on two or three students. Touch under each sound. Each student says all the sounds.)

EXERCISE 2
PRONUNCIATIONS

> **Note:** Do not write the words on the board. This is an oral exercise.

Task A

1. Listen: **mats**. Say it. (Signal.) *Mats*.
2. Next word: **mast**. Say it. (Signal.) *Mast*.
3. (Repeat step 2 for **cast, hams, meets, deeds**.)
4. (Repeat all the words until firm.)

Task B Men, fed, hen

1. I'll say words that have the sound **ĕĕĕ**. What sound? (Signal.) *ĕĕĕ*. Yes, **ĕĕĕ**.
2. (Repeat step 1 until firm.)
3. Listen: **men**. Your turn: **men**. Say it. (Signal.) *Men*. Yes, **men**.
4. Next word: **fed**. Say it. (Signal.) *Fed*. Yes, **fed**.
5. Next word: **hen**. Say it. (Signal.) *Hen*. Yes, **hen**.
6. (Repeat steps 3–5 until firm.)
7. What's the middle sound in the word **fffĕĕĕd**? (Signal.) *ĕĕĕ*. Yes, **ĕĕĕ**.
8. (Repeat step 7 until firm.)

Task C Mitt, met

1. Listen: **mitt**. Say it. (Signal.) *Mitt*.
2. Get ready to tell me the middle sound. Listen: **mmmĭĭĭt**. What's the middle sound? (Signal.) *ĭĭĭ*. Yes, **ĭĭĭ**.
3. Listen: **met**. Say it. (Signal.) *Met*.
4. Get ready to tell me the middle sound. Listen: **mmmĕĕĕt**. What's the middle sound? (Signal.) *ĕĕĕ*. Yes, **ĕĕĕ**.
5. One of those words has the middle sound **ĭĭĭ**. I'll say the words again: **mitt** (pause) **met**. Which word has the middle sound **ĭĭĭ**? (Signal.) *Mitt*. Yes, **mitt**.
6. Which word has the middle sound **ĕĕĕ**? (Signal.) *Met*. Yes, **met**.

Task D And, end

1. Listen: **and.** Say it. (Signal.) *And.*
   • **End.** Say it. (Signal.) *End.*
2. Get ready to tell me the first sound.
   Listen: **ăăănnnd.** What's the first sound?
   (Signal.) *ăăă.* Yes, **ăăă.**
3. Listen: **end.** Say it. (Signal.) *End.*
4. Get ready to tell me the first sound.
   Listen: **ĕĕĕnnnd.** What's the first sound?
   (Signal.) *ĕĕĕ.* Yes, **ĕĕĕ.**
5. One of those words has the first sound
   ĕĕĕ. I'll say the words again: **and** (pause)
   end. Which word has the first sound **ĕĕĕ?**
   (Signal.) *End.* Yes, **end.**
6. Which word has the first sound **ăăă?**
   (Signal.) *And.* Yes, **and.**

Task E Read, rod, rid

1. Listen: **read.** Say it. (Signal.) *Read.*
2. Get ready to tell me the middle sound.
   Listen: **rrrēēēd.** What's the middle sound?
   (Signal.) *ēēē.* Yes, **ēēē.**
3. Listen: **rod.** Say it. (Signal.) *Rod.*
4. Get ready to tell me the middle sound.
   Listen: **rrrŏŏŏd.** What's the middle
   sound? (Signal.) *ŏŏŏ.* Yes, **ŏŏŏ.**
5. Listen: **rid.** Say it. (Signal.) *Rid.*
6. Get ready to tell me the middle sound.
   Listen: **rrrĭĭĭd.** What's the middle sound?
   (Signal.) *ĭĭĭ.* Yes, **ĭĭĭ.**
7. One of those words has the middle sound
   ŏŏŏ. I'll say the words again: **read, rod,
   rid.** Which word has the middle sound
   ŏŏŏ? (Signal.) *Rod.* Yes, **rod.**
8. Which word has the middle sound **ēēē?**
   (Signal.) *Read.* Yes, **read.**
9. Which word has the middle sound **ĭĭĭ?**
   (Signal.) *Rid.* Yes, **rid.**

WORD READING

Task A

1. Read these words.
2. (Touch the ball of the arrow for **shot:**)
   Sound it out. Get ready. (Touch under
   sh, o, t:) *shshshŏŏŏt.* (Repeat until the
   students say the sounds without pausing.)
3. Again. Sound it out. Get ready. (Touch
   under **sh, o, t:**) *shshshŏŏŏt.*
   (Repeat until firm.)
4. (Touch the ball of the arrow:) Say it fast.
   (Slash right:) *Shot.* Yes, **shot.**
5. (Touch the ball of the arrow for **mats:**)
   Sound it out. Get ready. (Touch under **m,
   a, t, s:**) *mmmăăătsss.* (Repeat until the
   students say the sounds without pausing.)
6. Again. Sound it out. Get ready. (Touch
   under **m, a, t, s:**) *mmmăăătsss.*
   (Repeat until firm.)
7. (Touch the ball of the arrow:) Say it fast.
   (Slash right:) *Mats.* Yes, **mats.**
8. (Repeat steps 5–7 for remaining words.)

shot
→

mats
→

mash
→

math
→

mast
→

9. (Touch the ball of the arrow for **hash:**) Sound it out. Get ready. (Touch under **h, a, sh:**) *hăăăshshsh.* (Repeat until the students say the sounds without pausing.)

10. Again. Sound it out. Get ready. (Touch under **h, a, sh:**) *hăăăshshsh.* (Repeat until firm.)

11. (Touch the ball of the arrow:) Say it fast. (Slash right:) *Hash.* Yes, **hash.**

12. (Repeat steps 9–11 for remaining words.)

than

hams

hash

teeth

cash

that

cast

odd

meets

cod

deeds

not

nod

con

Task B **Word reading the fast way**

1. You're going to read these words the fast way.
2. (Touch the ball of the arrow for **hash.** Pause 4 seconds.) What word? (Slash right:) *Hash.*
3. (Touch the ball for **cash.** Pause 4 seconds.) What word? (Slash right:) *Cash.*
4. (Touch the ball for **cast.** Pause 4 seconds.) What word? (Slash right:) *Cast.*
5. (Repeat step 4 for **shot, that, not, nod, con.**)

hash

cash

cast

shot

that

not

nod

con

WORKBOOK EXERCISES

Note: Pass out the Workbooks. Direct the students to open to Lesson 22.

(Award 6 points if the group worked well during the word attack. Remind the students of the points they can earn in their Workbook.)

━━━━━ **EXERCISE 4** ━━━━━
NEW SOUND DICTATION

1. I'll say the sounds. You write the letters in part 1 in your Workbook.
2. First sound. (Pause.) **g.** What sound? (Signal.) *g.*
• Write it in the first blank.
   (Observe students and give feedback.)
3. Next sound. (Pause.) **fff.** What sound? (Signal.) *fff.*
• Write it.
   (Observe students and give feedback.)
4. (Repeat step 3 for **ŏŏŏ, mmm, ĭĭĭ, nnn, shshsh, ăăă, ēēē, thththth, fff, c.**)
5. (Repeat sounds students had trouble with.)

━━━━━ **EXERCISE 5** ━━━━━
WORD COMPLETION

1. Everybody, touch the first line in part 2 in your Workbook. ✓
2. You're going to write the word (pause) **it** on the first line. What word? (Signal.) *It.* Yes, **it.**
• Write (pause) **it** on the first line.
   (Observe students and give feedback.)
3. Now you're going to change (pause) **it** to say (pause) **fit.** Listen: **fit.** What is the first sound in (pause) **fit?** (Signal.) *fff.* Yes, **fff.**
• Fix it up to say **fit.**
   (Observe students and give feedback.)
4. Listen. You started with a word. What word? (Signal.) *It.*
• What word do you have now? (Signal.) *Fit.* Yes, **fit.**

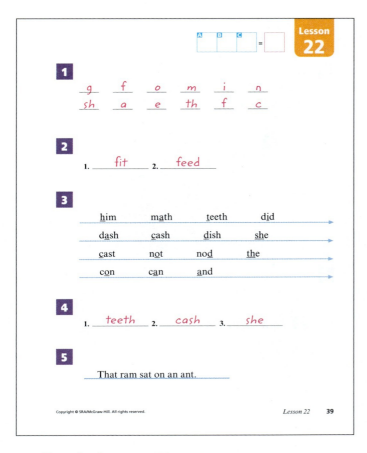

2. Touch the underlined part of the word. ✓
- What sound? (Signal.) *h.*

> **To correct sound errors:**
>   a. (Say the correct sound.)
>   b. (Repeat step 2 until firm.)

3. Figure out the word. (Pause.) What word? (Signal.) *Him.*

> **To correct word-reading errors:**
>   a. (Say the correct word.)
>   b. What word? (Signal.) Yes, _____.
>   c. Everybody, back to the first word in the row. ✓
>   d. (Repeat steps 2 and 3.)

4. Touch the underlined part of the next word. ✓
- What sound? (Signal.) *ăăă.*
5. Figure out the word. (Pause.) What word? (Signal.) *Math.*
6. Touch the underlined sound in the next word. (Pause.) What sound? (Signal.) *t.* (Pause.) What word? (Signal.) *Teeth.*
7. Touch the underlined sound in the next word. (Pause.) What sound? (Signal.) *ĭĭĭ.* (Pause.) What word? (Signal.) *Did.*
8. Touch the underlined sound in the next word. (Pause.) What sound? (Signal.) *ăăă.* (Pause.) What word? (Signal.) *Dash.*
9. (Repeat step 8 for **cash, dish, she, cast, not, nod, the, con, can, and.**)

━━━━━━ **EXERCISE 7** ━━━━━━

WORD COPYING

1. Everybody, touch part 4 in your Workbook. ✓
- You're going to write some of the words you just read.
2. The word you're going to write on the first line is **teeth.** What word? (Signal.) *Teeth.*
3. Find **teeth** and write it just as it is written in part 3.
(Observe students and give feedback.)

5. Touch the next line. ✓
- You're going to write the word (pause) **eed.** What word? (Signal.) *eed.* Yes, **eed.**
- Write (pause) **eed** on the line. Remember to write two ē's.
(Observe students and give feedback.)
6. Now you're going to change (pause) **eed** to say (pause) **feed.** Listen: **feed.** What is the first sound in (pause) **feed?** (Signal.) *fff.* Yes, **fff.**
- Fix it up to say **feed.**
(Observe students and give feedback.)
7. Listen. You started with a word. What word? (Signal.) *eed.*
- What word do you have now? (Signal.) *Feed.* Yes, **feed.**

━━━━━━ **EXERCISE 6** ━━━━━━

NEW WORD READING: Workbook

1. Touch the first word in part 3. ✓
- First you're going to tell me the sound of the underlined part. Then you're going to read the word the fast way.

4. The word you're going to write on the next line is **cash**. What word? (Signal.) *Cash.*
5. Find **cash** and write it just as it is written in part 3.
   (Observe students and give feedback.)
6. (Repeat steps 4 and 5 for **she**.)

─────── **EXERCISE 8** ───────

SENTENCE READING

Task A

1. Everybody, touch part 5. ✓
   - You're going to read each word in the sentence the fast way.
2. Touch under the first word. ✓
   - What word? (Signal.) *That.*
3. Next word. (Students touch under the next word.) ✓
   - What word? (Signal.) *Ram.*
4. (Repeat step 3 for **sat, on, an, ant.**)
5. (Repeat steps 2–4 until the students correctly identify all the words in the sentence in order.)

> **Individual test**
> Everybody, point to the first word in the sentence. (Call on a student.) Take your time. See if you can read all the words in this sentence the fast way without making a mistake. Everybody else, touch under the words that are read. (Call on different students to read the sentence.)

Task B

1. Everybody, touch the first word of the sentence. ✓
2. I'll read the sentence. Follow along. **That ram sat on an ant.**
3. Here are some questions:
   a. Everybody, who sat on the ant? (Signal.) *That ram.*
   b. What did the ram do? (Signal.) *Sat on an ant.*
   c. How do you think that ant felt? (Call on a student.) (Accept a reasonable response.)

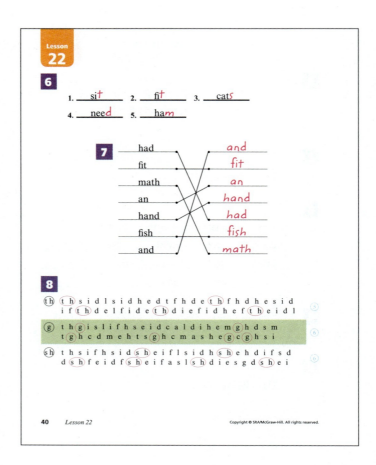

─────── **EXERCISE 9** ───────

WORD COMPLETION

1. Everybody, touch part 6. ✓
2. Sound out the word on the first line. Get ready. (Clap for **s, i:**) *sssĭĭ.*
   - What word? (Signal.) *si.* Yes, **si.**
3. Fix it up to say (pause) **sit.** (Pause.) **Sit.** What word? (Signal.) *Sit.* Yes, **sit.**
   - Fix it up.
     (Observe students and give feedback.)
4. Sound out the word on the next line. Get ready. (Clap for **f, i:**) *fffĭĭ.*
   - What word? (Signal.) *fi.* Yes, **fi.**
5. Fix it up to say (pause) **fit.** (Pause.) **Fit.** What word? (Signal.) *Fit.* Yes, **fit.**
   - Fix it up.
     (Observe students and give feedback.)
6. Sound out the word on the next line. Get ready. (Clap for **c, a, t:**) *cǎǎǎt.*
   - What word? (Signal.) *Cat.* Yes, **cat.**
7. Fix it up to say (pause) **cats.** (Pause.) **Cats.** What word? (Signal.) *Cats.* Yes, **cats.**
   - Fix it up.
     (Observe students and give feedback.)

8. Sound out the word on the next line. Get ready. (Clap for **n, ee:**) *nnnēēē.*
- What word? (Signal.) *nee.* Yes, **nee.**
9. Fix it up to say (pause) **need.** (Pause.) **Need.** What word? (Signal.) *Need.* Yes, **need.**
- Fix it up.
(Observe students and give feedback.)
10. Sound out the word on the next line. Get ready. (Clap for **h, a:**) *hăăă.*
- What word? (Signal.) *ha.* Yes, **ha.**
11. Fix it up to say (pause) **ham.** (Pause.) **Ham.** What word? (Signal.) *Ham.* Yes, **ham.**
- Fix it up.
(Observe students and give feedback.)

> **Individual test**
> I'll call on different students to read words in part 6. First word. (Call on a student.) What word? (Call on different students to read the remaining words.)

EXERCISE 10
MATCHING COMPLETION

1. Everybody, touch part 7. ✓
- Read the words the fast way.
2. Touch under the first word. ✓
- What word? (Signal.) *Had.*
3. Next word. ✓
- What word? (Signal.) *Fit.*
4. (Repeat step 3 for **math, an, hand, fish, and.**)
5. Later, you're going to write the words in the second column.

EXERCISE 11
CIRCLE GAME

1. Everybody, touch part 8. ✓
2. What will you circle in the first two lines? (Signal.) *ththth.*
3. What will you circle in the next two lines? (Signal.) *g.*
4. What will you circle in the last two lines? (Signal.) *shshsh.*
5. Circle the sounds and finish the rest of your Workbook lesson.

EXERCISE 12
WORKBOOK CHECK

1. (Check each student's Workbook.)
2. (Award points for Workbook performance.)
3. (Record the student's total points in Box B.)

0–2 errors	8 points
3–4 errors	4 points
5–6 errors	2 points
7 or more errors	0 points

INDIVIDUAL READING CHECKOUTS

EXERCISE 13
WORD-READING CHECKOUT

- Study the words in your Workbook. You'll each get a turn to read all these words the fast way. You can earn as many as 6 points for this reading.
- If you read all the words with no more than 1 error, you'll earn 6 points.
- If you make more than 1 error, you do not earn any points. But you'll have another chance to earn 6 points by studying the words some more and reading them again.
- (Check the students individually.)
- (Record either 6 or 0 points in Box C.)

Lesson point total
(Tell students to write the point total in the last box at the top of the Workbook page. Maximum for the lesson = 20 points.)

Point Summary Chart
(Tell students to write this point total in the box for Lesson 22 in the Point Summary Chart.)

END OF LESSON 22

Lesson 23

WORD-ATTACK SKILLS

EXERCISE 1
SOUND INTRODUCTION

1. (Point to **g:**) One sound this letter makes is **g**. What sound? (Touch.) *g*.
2. (Point to **ing:**) These letters usually make the sound **ing**. What sound? (Touch.) *ing*.
3. Say each sound when I touch it.
4. (Point to **g:**) What sound? (Touch under **g:**) *g*.
5. (Repeat step 4 for **ing, ŏ, g, s, th, ă, ĭ, ing, sh, ē**.)

g ing o
g s th
a i ing
sh e

Individual test
I'll call on different students to say all the sounds. If everybody I call on can say all the sounds without making a mistake, we'll go on to the next exercise. (Call on two or three students. Touch under each sound. Each student says all the sounds.)

EXERCISE 2
PRONUNCIATIONS

Note: Do not write the words on the board. This is an oral exercise.

Task A

1. Listen. She had a safety **pin**. (Pause.) **Pin**. Say it. (Signal.) *Pin*.
2. Next word. Listen. He wrote with a **pen**. (Pause.) **Pen**. Say it. (Signal.) *Pen*.
3. Next word: **least**. Say it. (Signal.) *Least*.
4. (Repeat step 3 for **last, list, cats, cast, rams, rims, sheets**.)
5. (Repeat all the words until firm.)

Task B Pen, ten, tell

1. I'll say words that have the sound **ĕĕĕ**. What sound? (Signal.) ĕĕĕ. Yes, ĕĕĕ.
2. (Repeat step 1 until firm.)
3. Listen: **pen**. Your turn: **pen**. Say it. (Signal.) *Pen*. Yes, **pen**.
4. Next word: **ten**. Say it. (Signal.) *Ten*. Yes, **ten**.
5. Next word: **tell**. Say it. (Signal.) *Tell*. Yes, **tell**.
6. (Repeat steps 3–5 until firm.)
7. What's the middle sound in the word **tĕĕĕlll?** (Signal.) ĕĕĕ. Yes, ĕĕĕ.
8. (Repeat step 7 until firm.)

Task C And, end

1. Listen. There were men **and** women. (Pause.) **And**. Say it. (Signal.) *And*.
2. Get ready to tell me the first sound. Listen: **ăăănnnd**. What's the first sound? (Signal.) ăăă. Yes, ăăă.
3. Listen. The story came to an **end**. (Pause.) **End**. Say it. (Signal.) *End*.
4. Get ready to tell me the first sound. Listen: **ĕĕĕnnnd**. What's the first sound? (Signal.) ĕĕĕ. Yes, ĕĕĕ.
5. One of those words has the first sound ĕĕĕ. I'll say the words again: **and** (pause) **end**. Which word has the first sound ĕĕĕ? (Signal.) *End*. Yes, **end**.
6. Which word has the first sound ăăă? (Signal.) *And*. Yes, **and**.

EXERCISE 3
NEW VOWEL VARIATIONS

1. (Point to **e** in **me**:) What sound? (Touch under **e**:) ēēē.
- (Touch the ball of the arrow. Pause.) What word? (Slash right:) *Me.*
2. (Point to **e** in **she**:) What sound? (Touch under **e**:) ēēē.
- (Touch the ball of the arrow. Pause.) What word? (Slash right:) *She.*
3. (Point to **e** in **he**:) What sound? (Touch under **e**:) ēēē.
- (Touch the ball of the arrow. Pause.) What word? (Slash right:) *He.*
4. (Point to **e** in **he**:) What sound does this letter make in all the words you just read? (Touch under **e**:) ēēē.
5. (Point to **e** in **met**:) This letter does not say ēēē in the words you're going to read now. This letter says ĕĕĕ.
- What sound? (Touch under **e**:) ĕĕĕ. (Repeat until firm.)
6. (Touch the ball of the arrow. Pause.) What word? (Slash right:) *Met.*

> **To correct, *met*, for example:**
> a. (Say:) **met.**
> - (Point to **e**:) What sound does this letter make in this word? (Touch under **e**:) ĕĕĕ.
> b. (Touch the ball of the arrow:) Sound it out. Get ready. (Touch under **m, e, t**:) mmmĕĕĕt. (Repeat until firm.)
> c. (Touch the ball of the arrow:) What word? (Signal.) *Met.*

7. (Point to **e** in **shed**:) What sound? (Touch under **e**:) ĕĕĕ.
- (Touch the ball of the arrow. Pause.) What word? (Slash right:) *Shed.*
8. (Point to **e** in **hen**:) What sound? (Touch under **e**:) ĕĕĕ.
- (Touch the ball of the arrow. Pause.) What word? (Slash right:) *Hen.*
9. (Repeat the list until the students can correctly identify all the words in order.)

me
she
he
met
shed
hen

EXERCISE 4
WORD READING

Task A

1. Read these words.
2. (Touch the ball of the arrow for **needs**:) Sound it out. Get ready. (Touch under **n, ee, d, s**:) nnnēēēdsss. (Repeat until the students say the sounds without pausing.)
3. Again. Sound it out. Get ready. (Touch under **n, ee, d, s**:) nnnēēēdsss. (Repeat until firm.)
4. (Touch the ball of the arrow:) Say it fast. (Slash right:) *Needs.* Yes, **needs.**

needs

5. (Touch the ball of the arrow for **than:**) Sound it out. Get ready. (Touch under **th, a, n:**) *thththăăănnn.* (Repeat until the students say the sounds without pausing.)
6. Again. Sound it out. Get ready. (Touch under **th, a, n:**) *thththăăănnn.* (Repeat until firm.)
7. (Touch the ball of the arrow:) Say it fast. (Slash right:) *Than.* Yes, **than.**
8. (Repeat steps 5–7 for **sing, shin, ring, ding.**)

than

sing

shin

ring

ding

Task B Word reading the fast way

1. You're going to read these words the fast way.
2. (Touch the ball of the arrow for **cats.** Pause 4 seconds.) What word? (Slash right:) *Cats.*
3. (Touch the ball for **cash.** Pause 4 seconds.) What word? (Slash right:) *Cash.*
4. (Touch the ball for **cast.** Pause 4 seconds.) What word? (Slash right:) *Cast.*
5. (Repeat step 4 for remaining words.)

cats

cash

cast

feet

him

tin

tan

did

cans

seem

6. (Touch the ball of the arrow for **not**. Pause 4 seconds.) What word? (Slash right:) *Not.*

7. (Repeat step 6 for remaining words.)

not

on

cod

WORKBOOK EXERCISES

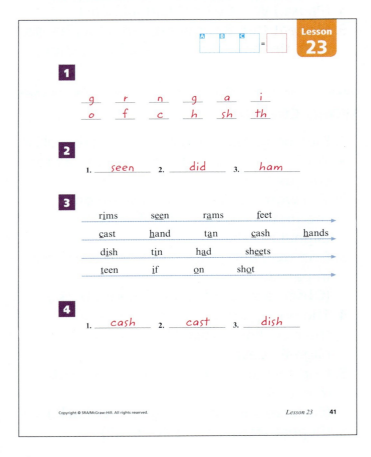

Note: Pass out the Workbooks. Direct the students to open to Lesson 23.

(Award 6 points if the group worked well during the word attack. Remind the students of the points they can earn in their Workbook.)

EXERCISE 5

SOUND DICTATION

1. I'll say the sounds. You write the letters in part 1 in your Workbook.
2. First sound. (Pause.) **g.** What sound? (Signal.) *g.*
   - Write it in the first blank.
     (Observe students and give feedback.)
3. Next sound. (Pause.) **rrr.** What sound? (Signal.) *rrr.*
   - Write it.
     (Observe students and give feedback.)
4. (Repeat step 3 for **nnn, g, ăăă, ĭĭĭ, ŏŏŏ, fff, c, h, shshsh, ththth.**)
5. (Repeat sounds students had trouble with.)

EXERCISE 6

WORD COMPLETION

1. Everybody, touch the first line in part 2 in your Workbook. ✓
2. You're going to write the word (pause) **een** on the first line. What word? (Signal.) *een.* Yes, **een.**
   - Write (pause) **een** on the first line.
     (Observe students and give feedback.)
3. Now you're going to change (pause) **een** to say (pause) **seen.**
   - Listen: **seen.** What is the first sound in (pause) **seen?** (Signal.) *sss.* Yes, **sss.**
   - Fix it up to say **seen.**
     (Observe students and give feedback.)
4. Listen. You started with a word. What word? (Signal.) *een.*
   - Yes, **een.** What word do you have now? (Signal.) *Seen.* Yes, **seen.**

5. Touch the next line. ✓
- You're going to write the word (pause) **id**. What word? (Signal.) *id.* Yes, **id**.
- Write (pause) **id** on the line.
  (Observe students and give feedback.)
6. Now you're going to change (pause) **id** to say (pause) **did**.
- Listen: **did**. What is the first sound in (pause) **did?** (Signal.) *d.* Yes, **d**.
- Fix it up to say **did**.
  (Observe students and give feedback.)
7. Listen. You started with a word. What word? (Signal.) *id.*
- What word do you have now? (Signal.) *Did.* Yes, **did**.
8. Touch the next line. ✓
- You're going to write the word (pause) **am**. What word? (Signal.) *Am.* Yes, **am**.
- Write (pause) **am** on the line.
  (Observe students and give feedback.)
9. Now you're going to change (pause) **am** to say (pause) **ham**.
- Listen: **ham**. What is the first sound in (pause) **ham?** (Signal.) *h.* Yes, **h**.
- Fix it up to say **ham**.
  (Observe students and give feedback.)
10. Listen. You started with a word. What word? (Signal.) *Am.*
- What word do you have now? (Signal.) *Ham.* Yes, **ham**.

================ EXERCISE 7 ================

WORD READING: Workbook

1. Touch the first word in part 3. ✓
- First you're going to tell me the sound of the underlined part. Then you're going to read the word the fast way.
2. Touch the underlined part of the word. ✓
- What sound? (Signal.) *ĩĩĩ.*

> **To correct sound errors:**
> a. (Say the correct sound.)
> b. (Repeat step 2 until firm.)

3. Figure out the word. (Pause.) What word? (Signal.) *Rims.*

> **To correct word-reading errors:**
> a. (Say the correct word.)
> b. What word? (Signal.) Yes, _____.
> c. Everybody, back to the first word in the row. ✓
> d. (Repeat steps 2 and 3.)

4. Touch the underlined part of the next word. ✓
- What sound? (Signal.) *ēēē.*
5. Figure out the word. (Pause.) What word? (Signal.) *Seen.*
6. Touch the underlined sound in the next word. (Pause.) What sound? (Signal.) *ăăă.*
- (Pause.) What word? (Signal.) *Rams.*
7. Touch the underlined sound in the next word. (Pause.) What sound? (Signal.) *fff.*
- (Pause.) What word? (Signal.) *Feet.*
8. Touch the underlined sound in the next word. (Pause.) What sound? (Signal.) *c.*
- (Pause.) What word? (Signal.) *Cast.*
9. (Repeat step 8 for **hand, tan, cash, hands, dish, tin, had, sheets, teen, if, on, shot**.)

================ EXERCISE 8 ================

WORD COPYING

1. Everybody, touch part 4 in your Workbook. ✓
- You're going to write some of the words you just read.
2. The word you're going to write on the first line is **cash**. What word? (Signal.) *Cash.*
3. Find **cash** and write it just as it is written in part 3.
   (Observe students and give feedback.)
4. The word you're going to write on the next line is **cast**. What word? (Signal.) *Cast.*
5. Find **cast** and write it just as it is written in part 3.
   (Observe students and give feedback.)
6. (Repeat steps 4 and 5 for **dish**.)

EXERCISE 9

NEW **SENTENCE READING**

Task A

1. Everybody, touch part 5. ✓
• You're going to read each word in these sentences the fast way.
2. Touch under the first word in sentence 1. ✓
• What word? (Signal.) *She.*
3. Next word. (Students touch under the next word.) ✓
• What word? (Signal.) *Has.*
4. Next word. (Students touch under the next word.) ✓
• What word? (Signal.) *Cats.*
5. (Repeat steps 2–4 until the students correctly identify all the words in the sentence in order.)
6. (Repeat steps 2–5 for each remaining sentence:
• 2. **He needs a tin dish.**
• 3. **It is in the hand.**)

Individual test
Everybody, point to the first word in sentence 1. (Call on a student.) Take your time. See if you can read all the words in this sentence the fast way without making a mistake. Everybody else, touch under the words that are read. (Give each student a chance to read one of the sentences.)

Task B

1. Everybody, touch sentence 2. ✓
• I'll read that sentence. Follow along. **He needs a tin dish.**
2. Here are some questions:
a. Everybody, what does he need? (Signal.) *A tin dish.*
b. What kind of dish does he need? (Signal.) *Tin.*
c. Who needs a tin dish? (Signal.) *He does.*

EXERCISE 10

WORD COMPLETION

1. Everybody, touch part 6. ✓
2. Sound out the word on the first line. Get ready. (Clap for **h, ee:**) *hēēē.*
• What word? (Signal.) *Hee.* Yes, **hee.**
3. Fix it up to say (pause) **heed.** (Pause.) **Heed.** What word? (Signal.) *Heed.* Yes, **heed.**
• Fix it up.
(Observe students and give feedback.)
4. Sound out the word on the next line. Get ready. (Clap for **th, a:**) *thththăăă.*
• What word? (Signal.) *tha.* Yes, **tha.**
5. Fix it up to say (pause) **than.** (Pause.) **Than.** What word? (Signal.) *Than.* Yes, **than.**
• Fix it up.
(Observe students and give feedback.)
6. Sound out the word on the third line. Get ready. (Clap for **d, i:**) *dĭĭĭ.*
• What word? (Signal.) *di.* Yes, **di.**
7. Fix it up to say (pause) **din.** (Pause.) **Din.** What word? (Signal.) *Din.* Yes, **din.**
• Fix it up.
(Observe students and give feedback.)
8. Sound out the word on the fourth line. Get ready. (Clap for **th, a:**) *thththăăă.*
• What word? (Signal.) *tha.* Yes, **tha.**
9. Fix it up to say (pause) **that.** (Pause.) **That.** What word? (Signal.) *That.* Yes, **that.**
• Fix it up.
(Observe students and give feedback.)

Individual test
I'll call on different students to read words in part 6. First word. (Call on a student.) What word? (Call on different students to read the remaining words.)

EXERCISE 11

MATCHING COMPLETION

1. Everybody, touch part 7. ✓
   • Read the words the fast way.
2. Touch under the first word. ✓
   • What word? (Signal.) *Mats.*
3. Next word. ✓
   • What word? (Signal.) *Had.*
4. (Repeat step 3 for **has, math, hand, mast.**)
5. Later, you're going to write the words in the second column.

EXERCISE 12

CIRCLE GAME

1. Everybody, touch part 8. ✓
2. What will you circle in the first two lines? (Signal.) *c.*
3. What will you circle in the next two lines? (Signal.) *ŏŏŏ.*
4. What will you circle in the last two lines? (Signal.) *ththth.*
5. Circle the sounds and finish the rest of your Workbook lesson.

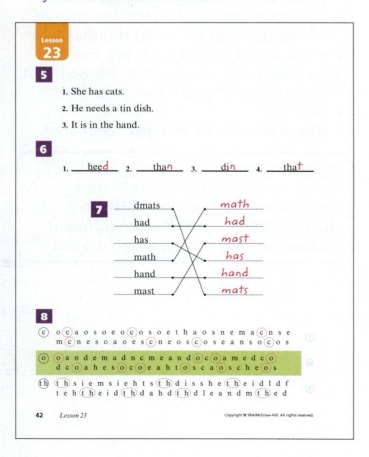

EXERCISE 13

WORKBOOK CHECK

1. (Check each student's Workbook.)
2. (Award points for Workbook performance.)
3. (Record the student's total points in Box B.)

0–2 errors	8 points
3–4 errors	4 points
5–6 errors	2 points
7 or more errors	0 points

INDIVIDUAL READING CHECKOUTS

EXERCISE 14

NEW SENTENCE-READING CHECKOUT

• Study the sentences in part 5. You'll each get a turn to read all these sentences. You can earn as many as 6 points for this reading.
• If you read all the sentences with no more than 1 error, you'll earn 6 points.
• If you make more than 1 error, you do not earn any points. But you'll have another chance to earn 6 points by studying the sentences some more and reading them again.
• (Check the students individually.)
• (Record either 6 or 0 points in Box C.)

Lesson point total

(Tell students to write the point total in the last box at the top of the Workbook page. Maximum for the lesson = 20 points.)

Point Summary Chart

(Tell students to write this point total in the box for Lesson 23 in the Point Summary Chart.)

END OF LESSON 23

WORD-ATTACK SKILLS

=== **EXERCISE 1** ===

SOUND IDENTIFICATION

1. Say each sound when I touch it.
2. (Point to **n:**) What sound? (Touch.) *nnn.* Yes, **nnn.**
3. (Repeat step 2 for **h, sh, th, f, ĭ, d, ă, ŏ, g.**)

n   **h**

sh   **th**

f   **i**   **d**

a   **o**   **g**

> **Individual test**
> I'll call on different students to say all the sounds. If everybody I call on can say all the sounds without making a mistake, we'll go on to the next exercise. (Call on two or three students. Touch under each sound. Each student says all the sounds.)

=== **EXERCISE 2** ===

PRONUNCIATIONS

> **Note:** Do not write the words on the board. This is an oral exercise.

Task A

1. Listen. **Send** me a letter. (Pause.) **Send.** Say it. (Signal.) *Send.*
2. Next word: **sand.** Say it. (Signal.) *Sand.*
3. (Repeat step 2 for **don, din, dean, reems, sheets.**)
4. (Repeat all the words until firm.)

Task B Pill, sit, pin

1. I'll say words that have the sound ĭĭĭ. What sound? (Signal.) *ĭĭĭ.* Yes, **ĭĭĭ.**
2. (Repeat step 1 until firm.)
3. Listen: **pill.** Your turn: **pill.** Say it. (Signal.) *Pill.* Yes, **pill.**
4. Next word: **sit.** Say it. (Signal.) *Sit.* Yes, **sit.**
5. Next word: **pin.** Say it. (Signal.) *Pin.* Yes, **pin.**
6. (Repeat steps 3–5 until firm.)
7. What's the middle sound in the word **pĭĭĭnnn?** (Signal.) *ĭĭĭ.* Yes, **ĭĭĭ.**
8. (Repeat step 7 until firm.)

Task C Pit, pet

1. Listen. The lion fell into a **pit.** (Pause.) **Pit.** Say it. (Signal.) *Pit.*
2. Get ready to tell me the middle sound. Listen: **pĭĭĭt.** What's the middle sound? (Signal.) *ĭĭĭ.* Yes, **ĭĭĭ.**
3. Listen. He had a **pet** dog. (Pause.) **Pet.** Say it. (Signal.) *Pet.*
4. Get ready to tell me the middle sound. Listen: **pĕĕĕt.** What's the middle sound? (Signal.) *ĕĕĕ.* Yes, **ĕĕĕ.**
5. One of those words has the middle sound ĭĭĭ. I'll say the words again: **pit** (pause) **pet.** Which word has the middle sound ĭĭĭ? (Signal.) *Pit.* Yes, **pit.**
6. Which word has the middle sound ĭĭĭ? (Signal.) *Pit.* Yes, **pit.**

Task D Teen, ten

1. Listen: **teen** (pause) **ten.** Say those words. (Signal.) *Teen, ten.* (Repeat until firm.)
2. One of those words has the middle sound ĕĕĕ. I'll say the words again: **teen** (pause) **ten.** Which word has the middle sound ĕĕĕ? (Signal.) *Ten.* Yes, **ten.**
3. Which word has the middle sound ēēē? (Signal.) *Teen.* Yes, **teen.**

Lesson 24

EXERCISE 3

VOWEL VARIATIONS

1. (Point to e in **he:**) What sound? (Touch under **e:**) ēēē.
- (Touch the ball of the arrow. Pause.) What word? (Slash right:) *He.*
2. (Point to e in **me:**) What sound? (Touch under **e:**) ēēē.
- (Touch the ball of the arrow. Pause.) What word? (Slash right:) *Me.*
3. (Point to e in **the:**) What sound? (Touch under **e:**) ēēē.
- (Touch the ball of the arrow. Pause.) What word? (Slash right:) *The.*
4. (Point to e in **she:**) What sound? (Touch under **e:**) ēēē.
- (Touch the ball of the arrow. Pause.) What word? (Slash right:) *She.*
5. (Point to e in **she:**) What sound does this letter make in all the words you just read? (Touch under **e:**) ēēē.
6. (Point to e in **hem:**) This letter does not say ēēē in the words you're going to read now. This letter says ĕĕĕ.
- What sound? (Touch under **e:**) ĕĕĕ. (Repeat until firm.)
7. (Touch the ball of the arrow. Pause.) What word? (Slash right:) *Hem.*

> To correct, *hem,* for example:
> a. (Say:) **hem.**
> - (Point to **e:**) What sound does this letter make in this word? (Touch under **e:**) ĕĕĕ.
> b. (Touch the ball of the arrow:) Sound it out. Get ready. (Touch under **h, e, m:**) hĕĕĕmmm. (Repeat until firm.)
> c. (Touch the ball of the arrow:) What word? (Signal.) *Hem.*

8. (Point to e in **shed:**) What sound? (Touch under **e:**) ĕĕĕ.
- (Touch the ball of the arrow. Pause.) What word? (Slash right:) *Shed.*
9. (Point to e in **men:**) What sound? (Touch under **e:**) ĕĕĕ.
- (Touch the ball of the arrow. Pause.) What word? (Slash right:) *Men.*

10. (Point to e in **them:**) What sound? (Touch under **e:**) ĕĕĕ.
- (Touch the ball of the arrow. Pause.) What word? (Slash right:) *Them.*
11. (Repeat the list until the students can correctly identify all the words in order.)

he

me

the

she

hem

shed

men

them

166 *Lesson 24*

EXERCISE 4
WORD READING

Task A

1. Read these words.
2. (Touch the ball of the arrow for **ring:**) Sound it out. Get ready. (Touch under **r, ing:**) *rrring.* (Repeat until the students say the sounds without pausing.)
3. Again. Sound it out. Get ready. (Touch under **r, ing:**) *rrring.* (Repeat until firm.)
4. (Touch the ball of the arrow:) Say it fast. (Slash right:) *Ring.* Yes, **ring.**
5. (Touch the ball of the arrow for **sing:**) Sound it out. Get ready. (Touch under **s, ing:**) *sssing.* (Repeat until the students say the sounds without pausing.)
6. Again. Sound it out. Get ready. (Touch under **s, ing:**) *sssing.* (Repeat until firm.)
7. (Touch the ball of the arrow:) Say it fast. (Slash right:) *Sing.* Yes, **sing.**
8. (Repeat steps 5–7 for **has, his.**)

ring
sing
has
his

Task B Word reading the fast way

1. You're going to read these words the fast way.
2. (Touch the ball of the arrow for **than.** Pause 4 seconds.) What word? (Slash right:) *Than.*
3. (Touch the ball for **fist.** Pause 4 seconds.) What word? (Slash right:) *Fist.*
4. (Touch the ball for **fits.** Pause 4 seconds.) What word? (Slash right:) *Fits.*
5. (Repeat step 4 for **fish, cast.**)

than
fist
fits
fish
cast

6. (Touch the ball of the arrow for **cash**. Pause 4 seconds.) What word? (Slash right:) *Cash.*
7. (Repeat step 6 for remaining words.)

cash
—————————————————▶

dim
—————————————————▶

din
—————————————————▶

did
—————————————————▶

not
—————————————————▶

con
—————————————————▶

WORKBOOK EXERCISES

> **Note:** Pass out the Workbooks. Direct the students to open to Lesson 24.

(Award 6 points if the group worked well during the word attack. Remind the students of the points they can earn in their Workbook.)

1

sh	g	th	i	n	c
a	o	f	n	h	t

2

1. ___tan___   2. ___rid___   3. ___cat___

3

mass	math	than	this	that
the	teeth	seems	mist	dad
feed	did	sheets	reefs	deed

4

1. ___that___   2. ___this___   3. ___than___

5

1. A shad can not sing.
2. Dad did math.
3. She can see that reef.

Lesson 24   **43**

EXERCISE 5

SOUND DICTATION

1. I'll say the sounds. You write the letters in part 1 in your Workbook.
2. First sound. (Pause.) **shshsh.** What sound? (Signal.) *shshsh.*
- Write it in the first blank. (Observe students and give feedback.)
3. Next sound. (Pause.) **g.** What sound? (Signal.) *g.*
- Write it. (Observe students and give feedback.)
4. (Repeat step 3 for **ththth, ĭĭĭ, nnn, c, ăăă, ŏŏŏ, fff, nnn, h, t.**)
5. (Repeat sounds students had trouble with.)

EXERCISE 6

WORD COMPLETION

1. Everybody, touch the first line in part 2 in your Workbook. ✓
2. You're going to write the word (pause) **an** on the first line. What word? (Signal.) *An.* Yes, **an.**
 • Write (pause) **an** on the first line. (Observe students and give feedback.)
3. Now you're going to change (pause) **an** to say (pause) **tan.**
 • Listen: **tan.** What is the first sound in (pause) **tan?** (Signal.) *t.* Yes, **t.**
 • Fix it up to say **tan.** (Observe students and give feedback.)
4. Listen. You started with a word. What word? (Signal.) *An.* Yes, **an.**
 • What word do you have now? (Signal.) *Tan.* Yes, **tan.**
5. Touch the next line. ✓
 • You're going to write the word (pause) **id.** What word? (Signal.) *id.* Yes, **id.**
 • Write (pause) **id** on the line. (Observe students and give feedback.)
6. Now you're going to change (pause) **id** to say (pause) **rid.**
 • Listen: **rid.** What is the first sound in (pause) **rid?** (Signal.) *r.* Yes, **r.**
 • Fix it up to say **rid.** (Observe students and give feedback.)
7. Listen. You started with a word. What word? (Signal.) *id.*
 • What word do you have now? (Signal.) *Rid.* Yes, **rid.**
8. Touch the next line. ✓
 • You're going to write the word (pause) **at.** What word? (Signal.) *At.* Yes, **at.**
 • Write (pause) **at** on the line. (Observe students and give feedback.)
9. Now you're going to change (pause) **at** to say (pause) **cat.**
 • Listen: **cat.** What is the first sound in (pause) **cat?** (Signal.) *c.* Yes, **c.**
 • Fix it up to say **cat.** (Observe students and give feedback.)

10. Listen. You started with a word. What word? (Signal.) *At.*
 • What word do you have now? (Signal.) *Cat.* Yes, **cat.**

EXERCISE 7

WORD READING: Workbook

1. Touch the first word in part 3. ✓
 • First you're going to tell me the sound of the underlined part. Then you're going to read the word the fast way.
2. Touch the underlined part of the word. ✓
 • What sound? (Signal.) *mmm.*

> **To correct sound errors:**
> a. (Say the correct sound.)
> b. (Repeat step 2 until firm.)

3. Figure out the word. (Pause.) What word? (Signal.) *Mass.*

> **To correct word-reading errors:**
> a. (Say the correct word.)
> b. What word? (Signal.) Yes, _____.
> c. Everybody, back to the first word in the row. ✓
> d. (Repeat steps 2 and 3.)

4. Touch the underlined sound in the next word. ✓
 • What sound? (Signal.) *ththth.*
 • What word? (Signal.) *Math.*
5. Touch the underlined sound in the next word. (Pause.) What sound? (Signal.) *ăăă.*
 • (Pause.) What word? (Signal.) *Than.*
6. Touch the underlined sound in the next word. (Pause.) What sound? (Signal.) *ĭĭĭ.*
 • (Pause.) What word? (Signal.) *This.*
7. (Repeat step 6 for **that, the, teeth, seems, mist, dad, feed, did, sheets, reefs, deed.**)

EXERCISE 8

WORD COPYING

1. Everybody, touch part 4 in your Workbook. ✓
• You're going to write some of the words you just read.
2. The word you're going to write on the first line is **that**. What word? (Signal.) *That*.
3. Find **that** and write it just as it is written in part 3.
(Observe students and give feedback.)
4. The word you're going to write on the next line is **this**. What word? (Signal.) *This*.
5. Find **this** and write it just as it is written in part 3.
(Observe students and give feedback.)
6. (Repeat steps 4 and 5 for **than**.)

EXERCISE 9

SENTENCE READING

Task A

1. Everybody, touch part 5. ✓
• You're going to read each word in these sentences the fast way.
2. Touch under the first word in sentence 1. ✓
• What word? (Signal.) *A*.
3. Next word. (Students touch under the next word.) ✓
• What word? (Signal.) *Shad*.
• A shad is a fish.
4. What's a shad? (Signal.) *A fish*.
5. Go back to the first word in sentence 1.
6. (Repeat steps 2 and 3 until the students correctly identify all the words in the sentence in order.)
7. (Repeat steps 2, 3 and 6 for each remaining sentence:
• **2. Dad did math.**
• **3. She can see that reef.**)

Individual test
Everybody, point to the first word in sentence 1. (Call on a student.) Take your time. See if you can read all the words in this sentence the fast way without making a mistake. Everybody else, touch under the words that are read. (Give each student a chance to read one of the sentences.)

Task B

1. Everybody, touch sentence 1. ✓
• I'll read that sentence. Follow along. **A shad can not sing.**
2. Here are some questions:
   a. A shad is a fish. Everybody, a shad can not do what? (Signal.) *Sing*.
   b. What can't sing? (Signal.) *A shad*.

EXERCISE 10

WORD COMPLETION

1. Everybody, touch part 6. ✓
2. Sound out the word on the first line. Get ready. (Clap for **sh, ee:**) *shshshēēē*.
• What word? (Signal.) *shee*. Yes, **shee**.
3. Fix it up to say (pause) **sheet**. (Pause.) **Sheet**. What word? (Signal.) *Sheet*. Yes, **sheet**.
• Fix it up.
(Observe students and give feedback.)
4. Sound out the word on the next line. Get ready. (Clap for **m, i, s:**) *mmmĭĭĭsss*.
• What word? (Signal.) *mis*. Yes, **mis**.
5. Fix it up to say (pause) **mist**. (Pause.) **Mist**. What word? (Signal.) *Mist*. Yes, **mist**.
• Fix it up.
(Observe students and give feedback.)
6. Sound out the word on the third line. Get ready. (Clap for **f, a, s:**) *fffăăăsss*.
• What word? (Signal.) *fas*. Yes, **fas**.
7. Fix it up to say (pause) **fast**. (Pause.) **Fast**. What word? (Signal.) *Fast*. Yes, **fast**.
• Fix it up.
(Observe students and give feedback.)
8. Sound out the word on the fourth line. Get ready. (Clap for **h, a:**) *hăăă*.
• What word? (Signal.) *ha*. Yes, **hă**.
9. Fix it up to say (pause) **had**. (Pause.) **Had**. What word? (Signal.) *Had*. Yes, **had**.
• Fix it up.
(Observe students and give feedback.)

Individual test
I'll call on different students to read words in part 6. First word. (Call on a student.) What word? (Call on different students to read the remaining words.)

EXERCISE 11
MATCHING COMPLETION

1. Everybody, touch part 7. ✓
• Read the words the fast way.
2. Touch under the first word. ✓
• What word? (Signal.) *Mast.*
3. Next word. ✓
• What word? (Signal.) *That.*
4. (Repeat step 3 for **mats, math, than, fits.**)
5. Later, you're going to write the words in the second column.

EXERCISE 12
CIRCLE GAME

1. Everybody, touch part 8. ✓
2. What will you circle in the first two lines? (Signal.) *fff.*
3. What will you circle in the next two lines? (Signal.) *ththth.*
4. What will you circle in the last two lines? (Signal.) *g.*
5. Circle the sounds and finish the rest of your Workbook lesson.

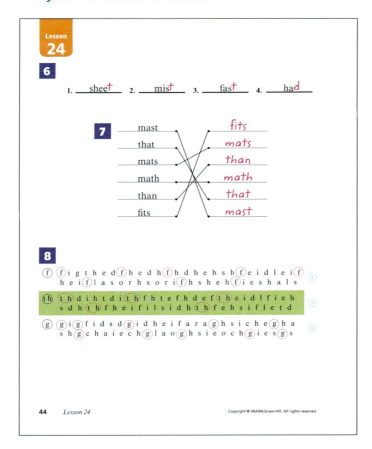

EXERCISE 13
WORKBOOK CHECK

1. (Check each student's Workbook.)
2. (Award points for Workbook performance.)
3. (Record the student's total points in Box B.)

0–2 errors	8 points
3–4 errors	4 points
5–6 errors	2 points
7 or more errors	0 points

INDIVIDUAL READING CHECKOUTS

EXERCISE 14
SENTENCE-READING CHECKOUT

• Study the sentences in part 5. You'll each get a turn to read all these sentences. You can earn as many as 6 points for this reading.
• If you read all the sentences with no more than 1 error, you'll earn 6 points.
• If you make more than 1 error, you do not earn any points. But you'll have another chance to earn 6 points by studying the sentences some more and reading them again.
• (Check the students individually.)
• (Record either 6 or 0 points in Box C.)

Lesson point total

(Tell students to write the point total in the last box at the top of the Workbook page. Maximum for the lesson = 20 points.)

Point Summary Chart

(Tell students to write this point total in the box for Lesson 24 in the Point Summary Chart.)

END OF LESSON 24

WORD-ATTACK SKILLS

──────── **EXERCISE 1** ────────
NEW **SOUND INTRODUCTION**

1. (Point to **e:**) Listen. You learned two sounds for this letter. One sound is the letter name. That's *ēēē*. You say *ēēē* when you say the alphabet. The other sound is *ĕĕĕ*. That's not the letter name. Your turn.
2. One sound is the letter name. What's that sound? (Touch.) *ēēē*. Yes, *ēēē*.
• And what's the other sound? (Touch.) *ĕĕĕ*. Yes, *ĕĕĕ*.
3. (Repeat step 2 until firm.)
4. Say each sound when I touch it.
5. (Point to **th:**) What sound? (Touch.) *ththth*. Yes, **ththth**.
6. (Repeat step 5 for **s, ă, c, sh, t, ĭ, g, ŏ, r, f.**)

┌─────────────────────────────────────┐
Individual test
I'll call on different students to say all the sounds. If everybody I call on can say all the sounds without making a mistake, we'll go on to the next exercise. (Call on two or three students. Touch under each sound. Each student says all the sounds.)
└─────────────────────────────────────┘

e th
s a c
sh t i
g o r f

EXERCISE 2

VOWEL VARIATIONS

1. (Point to **e** in **shed:**) What sound? (Touch under **e:**) ĕĕĕ.
- (Touch the ball of the arrow. Pause.) What word? (Slash right:) *Shed.*
2. (Point to **e** in **them:**) What sound? (Touch under **e:**) ĕĕĕ.
- (Touch the ball of the arrow. Pause.) What word? (Slash right:) *Them.*
3. (Point to **e** in **met:**) What sound? (Touch under **e:**) ĕĕĕ.
- (Touch the ball of the arrow. Pause.) What word? (Slash right:) *Met.*
4. (Point to **e** in **hen:**) What sound? (Touch under **e:**) ĕĕĕ.
- (Touch the ball of the arrow. Pause.) What word? (Slash right:) *Hen.*
5. (Point to **e** in **hen:**) What sound does this letter make in all the words you just read? (Touch under **e:**) ĕĕĕ.

shed

them

met

hen

6. (Point to **e** in **she:**) This letter does not say ĕĕĕ in the words you're going to read now. This letter says ēēē. What sound? (Touch under **e.**) ēēē. (Repeat until firm.)
7. (Touch the ball of the arrow. Pause.) What word? (Slash right:) *She.*

To correct, *she,* for example:
a. (Say:) **she.**
- (Point to **e:**) What sound does this letter make in this word? (Touch under **e:**) ēēē.
b. (Touch the ball of the arrow:) Sound it out. Get ready. (Touch under **sh, e:**) shshshēēē. (Repeat until firm.)
c. (Touch the ball of the arrow:) What word? (Signal.) *She.*

8. (Point to **e** in **the:**) What sound? (Touch under **e:**) ēēē.
- (Touch the ball of the arrow. Pause.) What word? (Slash right:) *The.*
9. (Point to **e** in **me:**) What sound? (Touch under **e:**) ēēē.
- (Touch the ball of the arrow. Pause.) What word? (Slash right:) *Me.*
10. (Point to **e** in **he:**) What sound? (Touch under **e:**) ēēē.
- (Touch the ball of the arrow. Pause.) What word? (Slash right:) *He.*
11. (Repeat both lists until the students can correctly identify all the words in order.)

she

the

me

he

EXERCISE 3

PRONUNCIATIONS

> **Note:** Do not write the words on the board. This is an oral exercise.

Task A

1. Listen. The tree will **bend.** (Pause.) **Bend.** Say it. (Signal.) *Bend.*
2. Next word. Listen. We will listen to the **band.** (Pause.) **Band.** Say it. (Signal.) *Band.*
3. Next word: **din.** Say it. (Signal.) *Din.*
4. Next word. Listen. The bear slept in its **den.** (Pause.) **Den.** Say it. (Signal.) *Den.*
5. Next word: **cats.** Say it. (Signal.) *Cats.*
6. (Repeat step 5 for **cast, sheets, mats, math.**)
7. (Repeat all the words until firm.)

Task B Den, set, fell

1. I'll say words that have the sound **ĕĕĕ.** What sound? (Signal.) *ĕĕĕ.* Yes, **ĕĕĕ.**
2. (Repeat step 1 until firm.)
3. Listen: **den, set, fell.** Your turn: **den.** Say it. (Signal.) *Den.* Yes, **den.**
4. Next word: **set.** Say it. (Signal.) *Set.* Yes, **set.**
5. Next word: **fell.** Say it. (Signal.) *Fell.* Yes, **fell.**
6. (Repeat steps 3–5 until firm.)
7. What's the middle sound in the word **sssĕĕĕt?** (Signal.) *ĕĕĕ.* Yes, **ĕĕĕ.**
8. (Repeat step 7 until firm.)

Task C Rod, red

1. Listen: **rod.** Say it. (Signal.) *Rod.*
2. Get ready to tell me the middle sound. Listen: **rrrŏŏŏd.** What's the middle sound? (Signal.) *ŏŏŏ.* Yes, **ŏŏŏ.**
3. Listen: **red.** Say it. (Signal.) *Red.*
4. Get ready to tell me the middle sound. Listen: **rrrĕĕĕd.** What's the middle sound? (Signal.) *ĕĕĕ.* Yes, **ĕĕĕ.**
5. One of those words has the middle sound **ŏŏŏ.** I'll say the words again: **rod** (pause) **red.** Which word has the middle sound **ŏŏŏ?** (Signal.) *Rod.* Yes, **rod.**
6. Which word has the middle sound **ĕĕĕ?** (Signal.) *Red.* Yes, **red.**

Task D Tell, till

1. Listen. I will do what you **tell** me. (Pause.) **Tell.** Say it. (Signal.) *Tell.*
2. Get ready to tell me the middle sound. Listen: **tĕĕĕlll.** What's the middle sound? (Signal.) *ĕĕĕ.* Yes, **ĕĕĕ.**
3. Listen: Wait **till** I get there. (Pause.) **Till.** Say it. (Signal.) *Till.*
4. Get ready to tell me the middle sound. Listen: **tĭĭĭlll.** What's the middle sound? (Signal.) *ĭĭĭ.* Yes, **ĭĭĭ.**
5. One of those words has the middle sound **ĭĭĭ.** I'll say the words again: **tell** (pause) **till.** Which word has the middle sound **ĭĭĭ?** (Signal.) *Till.* Yes, **till.**
6. Which word has the middle sound **ĕĕĕ?** (Signal.) *Tell.* Yes, **tell.**

EXERCISE 4

NEW WORD READING THE FAST WAY

1. You're going to read the words the fast way.
2. (Touch the ball of the arrow for **sing.** Pause 4 seconds.) What word? (Slash right:) *Sing.*
3. (Touch the ball for **ding.** Pause 4 seconds.) What word? (Slash right:) *Ding.*
4. (Touch the ball for **has.** Pause 4 seconds.) What word? (Slash right:) *Has.*

sing
→

ding
→

has
→

5. (Touch the ball for **as.** Pause 4 seconds.)
   What word? (Slash right:) *As.*
6. (Repeat step 5 for each remaining word.)

as

his

is

feed

not

got

mod

mad

mid

sham

fast

mist

meets

fist

dish

WORKBOOK EXERCISES

Note: Pass out the Workbooks. Direct the students to open to Lesson 25.

(Award 6 points if the group worked well during the word attack. Remind the students of the points they can earn in their Workbook.)

───────── **EXERCISE 5** ─────────
SOUND DICTATION

1. I'll say the sounds. You write the letters in part 1 in your Workbook.
2. First sound. (Pause.) **fff.** What sound? (Signal.) *fff.*
   • Write it in the first blank. (Observe students and give feedback.)
3. Next sound. (Pause.) **k.** What sound? (Signal.) *k.*
   • Write it. (Observe students and give feedback.)
4. (Repeat step 3 for **d, h, shshsh, thththth, ĭĭĭ, g, ăăă, ŏŏŏ, ēēē, nnn.**)
5. (Repeat sounds students had trouble with.)

───────── **EXERCISE 6** ─────────
WORD COMPLETION

1. Everybody, touch the first line in part 2 in your Workbook. ✓
2. You're going to write the word (pause) **ot** on the first line. What word? (Signal.) *ot.* Yes, **ot.**
   • Write (pause) **ot** on the first line. (Observe students and give feedback.)
3. Now you're going to change (pause) **ot** to say (pause) **hot.**
   • Listen: **hot.** What is the first sound in (pause) **hot?** (Signal.) *h.* Yes, **h.**
   • Fix it up to say **hot.** (Observe students and give feedback.)
4. Listen. You started with a word. What word? (Signal.) *ot.*
   • What word do you have now? (Signal.) *Hot.* Yes, **hot.**

176 *Lesson 25*

A | B | C | = |

1

f c d h sh th
i g a o e n

2

1. hot   2. can   3. feet

3

cats	sheets	cast	math
mats	dam	sees	feet
feed	dim	din	dan

4

1. feed   2. math   3. mats

5

1. She had a shad.
2. That dash is fast.
3. He has rats and cats.

Lesson 25 **45**

5. Touch the next line. ✓
   • You're going to write the word (pause) **an.** What word? (Signal.) *An.* Yes, **an.**
   • Write (pause) **an** on the line. (Observe students and give feedback.)
6. Now you're going to change (pause) **an** to say (pause) **can.**
   • Listen: **can.** What is the first sound in (pause) **can?** (Signal.) *c.* Yes, **c.**
   • Fix it up to say **can.** (Observe students and give feedback.)
7. Listen. You started with a word. What word? (Signal.) *An.* What word do you have now? (Signal.) *Can.* Yes, **can.**
8. Touch the third line. ✓
   • You're going to write the word (pause) **eet.** What word? (Signal.) *eet.* Yes, **eet.**
   • Write (pause) **eet** on the line. Remember to write two **ēs.** (Observe students and give feedback.)
9. Now you're going to change (pause) **eet** to say (pause) **feet.**
   • Listen: **feet.** What is the first sound in (pause) **feet?** (Signal.) *fff.* Yes, **fff.**
   • Fix it up to say **feet.** (Observe students and give feedback.)

10. Listen. You started with a word. What word? (Signal.) *eet.* What word do you have now? (Signal.) *Feet. Yes,* **feet.**

======== **EXERCISE 7** ========

NEW **WORD READING: Workbook**

1. Touch the first word in part 3. ✓
- Tell me the sound for the underlined part. Then tell me the word.
2. Touch the underlined sound in the first word. (Pause.) What sound? (Signal.) *sss.*
- (Pause.) What word? (Signal.) *Cats.*
3. Touch the underlined sound in the next word. (Pause.) What sound? (Signal.) *sss.*
- (Pause.) What word? (Signal.) *Sheets.*
4. (Repeat step 3 for **ca̲st, ma̲th, mats̲, da̲m, s̲ees, fee̲t, fee̲d, di̲m, di̲n, da̲n.**)

======== **EXERCISE 8** ========

WORD COPYING

1. Everybody, touch part 4 in your Workbook. ✓
- You're going to write some of the words you just read.
2. The word you're going to write on the first line is **feed.** What word? (Signal.) *Feed.*
3. Find **feed** and write it just as it is written in part 3.
   (Observe students and give feedback.)
4. The word you're going to write on the next line is **math.** What word? (Signal.) *Math.*
5. Find **math** and write it just as it is written in part 3.
   (Observe students and give feedback.)
6. (Repeat steps 4 and 5 for **mats.**)

======== **EXERCISE 9** ========

SENTENCE READING

Task A

1. Everybody, touch part 5. ✓
- You're going to read each word in these sentences the fast way.
2. Touch the first word in sentence 1. ✓
- What word? (Signal.) *She.*

3. Next word. (Students touch under the next word.) ✓
- What word? (Signal.) *Had.*
4. (Repeat step 3 for **a, shad.**)
5. (Repeat steps 2–4 until the students can correctly identify all the words in the sentence order.)
6. (Repeat steps 2–5 for each remaining sentence:
- **2. That dash is fast.**
- **3. He has rats and cats.**)

> **Individual test**
> Everybody, point to the first word in sentence 1. (Call on a student.) Take your time. See if you can read all the words in this sentence the fast way without making a mistake. Everybody else, touch under the words that are read. (Give each student a chance to read one of the sentences.)

Task B

1. Everybody, touch sentence 2. ✓
- I'll read that sentence. Follow along. **That dash is fast.**
2. Here are some questions:
   a. What is a dash? (Call on a student.) (Idea: *A short race.*)
   b. What does it mean to say that a dash is fast? (Call on a student.) (Idea: *The runners move fast.*)

======== **EXERCISE 10** ========

WORD COMPLETION

1. Everybody, touch part 6. ✓
2. Sound out the word on the first line. Get ready. (Clap for **d, a:**) *dăăă.*
- What word? (Signal.) *da. Yes,* **da.**
3. Fix it up to say (pause) **dash.** (Pause.) **Dash.** What word? (Signal.) *Dash. Yes,* **dash.**
- Fix it up.
   (Observe students and give feedback.)
4. Sound out the word on the next line. Get ready. (Clap for **th, a:**) *thththăăă.*
- What word? (Signal.) *tha. Yes,* **tha.**

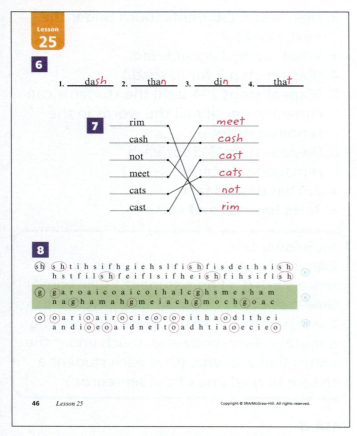

5. Fix it up to say (pause) **than.** (Pause.)
   Than. What word? (Signal.) *Than.*
   Yes, **than.**
• Fix it up.
   (Observe students and give feedback.)
6. Sound out the word on the third line.
   Get ready. (Clap for **d, i:**) *dĭĭĭ.*
• What word? (Signal.) *di.* Yes, **di.**
7. Fix it up to say (pause) **din.** (Pause.) **Din.**
   What word? (Signal.) *Din.* Yes, **din.**
• Fix it up.
   (Observe students and give feedback.)
8. Sound out the word on the fourth line.
   Get ready. (Clap for **th, a:**) *thththăăă.*
• What word? (Signal.) *tha.* Yes, **tha.**
9. Fix it up to say (pause) **that.** (Pause.) **That.**
   What word? (Signal.) *That.* Yes, **that.**
• Fix it up.
   (Observe students and give feedback.)

> **Individual test**
> I'll call on different students to read
> words. First word. (Call on a student.)
> What word? (Call on different students to
> read the remaining words.)

EXERCISE 11

MATCHING COMPLETION

1. Everybody, touch part 7. ✓
• Read the words the fast way.
2. Touch under the first word. ✓
• What word? (Signal.) *Rim.*
3. Next word. ✓
• What word? (Signal.) *Cash.*
4. (Repeat step 3 for **not, meet, cats, cast.**)
5. Later, you're going to write the words in
   the second column.

EXERCISE 12

CIRCLE GAME

1. Everybody, touch part 8. ✓
2. What will you circle in the first two lines?
   (Signal.) *shshsh.*
3. What will you circle in the next two lines?
   (Signal.) *g.*
4. What will you circle in the last two lines?
   (Signal.) *ŏŏŏ.*
5. Circle the sounds and finish the rest of
   your Workbook lesson.

EXERCISE 13

WORKBOOK CHECK

1. (Check each student's Workbook.)
2. (Award points for Workbook performance.)
3. (Record the student's total points in Box B.)

0–2 errors	8 points
3–4 errors	4 points
5–6 errors	2 points
7 or more errors	0 points

INDIVIDUAL READING CHECKOUTS

━━━━━ **EXERCISE 14** ━━━━━

SENTENCE-READING CHECKOUT

- Study the sentences in part 5. You'll each get a turn to read all these sentences. You can earn as many as 6 points for this reading.
- If you read all the sentences with no more than 1 error, you'll earn 6 points.
- If you make more than 1 error, you do not earn any points. But you'll have another chance to earn 6 points by studying the sentences some more and reading them again.
- (Check the students individually.)
- (Record either 6 or 0 points in Box C.)

Lesson point total

(Tell students to write the point total in the last box at the top of the Workbook page. Maximum for the lesson = 20 points.)

Point Summary Chart

(Tell students to write this point total in the box for Lesson 25 in the Point Summary Chart.)

Five-lesson point summary

(Tell students to add the point totals for Lessons 21 through 25 in the Point Summary Chart and to write the total for Block 5. Maximum for Block 5 = 100 points.)

END OF LESSON 25

MASTERY TEST 6
━ AFTER LESSON 25, BEFORE LESSON 26 ━

> **Note:** Test each student individually. Administer the test so that other students do not overhear the student being tested.

Part A Vowel variations: ē

1. First tell me the sound the letter makes in the word and then tell me the word.
2. (Point to **e** in **me:**) What sound? (Touch.) ēēē.
3. (Test item. Touch the ball of the arrow for **me:**) What word? (Slash right:) *Me.*
4. (Repeat steps 2 and 3 for **the, she.**)

me ●————————————▶

the ●————————————▶

she ●————————————▶

Part B Vowel variations: ĕ

1. (Point to **e** in **met:**) This letter does not say ēēē in the words you're going to read now.
2. (Point to **e** in **met:**) This letter says ĕĕĕ. What sound? (Touch.) ĕĕĕ.
3. (Test item. Touch the ball of the arrow for **met:**) What word? (Slash right:) *Met.*
4. (Repeat steps 2 and 3 for **them, shed.**)

met ●————————————▶

them ●————————————▶

shed ●————————————▶

Scoring the test

1. (Count each student's errors on the test. Write these numbers in the Test 6 boxes on the *Decoding A* Mastery Test Student Profile form. Circle **P** or **F**.)
2. (When all students have been tested, record each student's **P** or **F** score on the *Decoding A* Mastery Test Group Summary form under Test 6. Reproducible summary forms are at the back of the Teacher's Guide.)
 • (Pass criterion: 0 errors. Circle **P**.)
 • (Fail criterion: 1 or more errors. Circle **F**.)

Remedies

(If more than 25 percent of the students missed any words in part 1 or 2, repeat Lessons 24 and 25. Permission is granted to reproduce the Workbook pages for these lessons for classroom use. Then retest.)

Lesson Objectives	LESSON 26 Exercise	LESSON 27 Exercise	LESSON 28 Exercise	LESSON 29 Exercise	LESSON 30 Exercise
Word Attack					
Phonemic Awareness					
Sound/Word Pronunciation	1–3	1–3	1–3	1–3	1–3
Identify Sounds in Words	2, 3	2, 3	2, 3	2, 3	2, 3
Decoding and Word Analysis					
Letter Sounds: ĕ, ē, th, m, h, s, i, o, a, n, sh, g, ing	1				
Letter Sounds: c, k, ck, ĕ, ē, i, r, sh, th, g, ing, o, a		1			
Letter Sounds: c, k, ck, e, a, ing, i, g, d, o, th			1		
Letter Sounds: ĕ, ē, c, ck, th, a, sh, i, o, g				1	
Letter Sounds: ĕ, ē, ing, th, a, i, o sh, s, r, d, h, m, n					1
Vowel Sound Discrimination: ē, e	3	2	2	2	3
Sounding Out/Blending					
Word Recognition	4	4	4	4	4
Assessment					
Ongoing: Individual Tests	1	1	1	1	1
Formal: Mastery Test					MT 7
Group Reading					
Decoding and Word Analysis					
Read Decodable Text					11
Comprehension					
Draw Inferences					11
Note Details					11
Assessment					
Ongoing: Comprehension Check					11
Ongoing: Decoding Accuracy					11
Workbook Exercises					
Decoding and Word Analysis					
Word Recognition	8	8	8	8	8
Sentence Reading	9	9	9	9	9
Sound Combinations	8	8	8	8	8
Spelling: Sound/Letter Relationships	6, 7, 10, 11	6, 7, 10, 11	6, 7, 10, 11	6, 7, 10, 11	6, 7, 10, 12
Spelling: CVC, CCV	5	5	5		
Spelling: CVC, CCV, CV					5
Spelling: CVC, CCV, CV, CCVC				5	
Visual Discrimination	11, 12	11, 12	11, 12	11, 12	12, 13
Assessment					
Ongoing: Individual Tests	9, 10	9, 10	9, 10	9, 10	9, 10
Ongoing: Teacher-Monitored Accuracy	14	14	14	14	15
Ongoing: Workcheck	13	13	13	13	14

WORD-ATTACK SKILLS

EXERCISE 1
SOUND IDENTIFICATION

1. (Point to **e:**) One sound you learned for this letter is the letter name. Everybody, what's that sound? (Touch.) *ēēē*. Yes, **ēēē**.
   - What's the other sound? (Touch.) *ĕĕĕ*. Yes, **ĕĕĕ**.
2. Say each sound when I touch it.
3. (Point to **th:**) What sound? (Touch.) *ththth*. Yes, **ththth**.
4. (Repeat step 3 for **m, h, s, ĭ, ŏ, ă, n, sh, g, ing.**)

e   th   m

h   s   i   o

a   n   sh

g   ing

> **Individual test**
> I'll call on different students to say all the sounds. If everybody I call on can say all the sounds without making a mistake, we'll go on to the next exercise. (Call on two or three students. Touch under each sound. Each student says all the sounds.)

EXERCISE 2
PRONUNCIATIONS

> **Note:** Do not write the words on the board. This is an oral exercise.

Task A

1. Listen: **cat.** Say it. (Signal.) *Cat.*
2. Next word: **kit.** Say it. (Signal.) *Kit.*
3. (Repeat step 2 for **cot, fits, hams, mats.**)
4. (Repeat all the words until firm.)

Task B Sit, in, him

1. I'll say words that have the sound *ĭĭĭ*. What sound? (Signal.) *ĭĭĭ*. Yes, **ĭĭĭ**.
2. (Repeat step 1 until firm.)
3. Listen: **sit, in, him.** Your turn: **sit.** Say it. (Signal.) *Sit.* Yes, **sit**.
4. Next word: **in.** Say it. (Signal.) *In.* Yes, **in**.
5. Next word: **him.** Say it. (Signal.) *Him.* Yes, **him**.
6. (Repeat steps 3–5 until firm.)
7. What's the first sound in the word *ĭĭĭnnn?* (Signal.) *ĭĭĭ*. Yes, **ĭĭĭ**.
8. (Repeat step 7 until firm.)

Task C Hem, him

1. Listen. She had a **hem** in her skirt. (Pause.) **Hem.** Say it. (Signal.) *Hem.*
2. Get ready to tell me the middle sound. Listen: **hĕĕĕmmm.** What's the middle sound? (Signal.) *ĕĕĕ*. Yes, **ĕĕĕ**.
3. Listen. We like **him.** (Pause.) **Him.** Say it. (Signal.) *Him.*
4. Get ready to tell me the middle sound. Listen: **hĭĭĭmmm.** What's the middle sound? (Signal.) *ĭĭĭ*. Yes, **ĭĭĭ**.
5. One of those words has the middle sound **ĕĕĕ**. I'll say the words again: **hem** (pause) **him.** Which word has the middle sound **ĕĕĕ?** (Signal.) *Hem.* Yes, **hem**.
6. Which word has the middle sound **ĭĭĭ?** (Signal.) *Him.* Yes, **him**.

Task D **Man, men**

1. Listen. I see only one **man.** (Pause.) **Man.**
   Say it. (Signal.) *Man.*
   - Listen. I see two **men.** (Pause.) **Men.** Say
     it. (Signal.) *Men.*
2. One of those words has the middle sound
   ăăă. I'll say the words again: **man** (pause)
   men.
3. Which word has the middle sound **ăăă?**
   (Signal.) *Man.* Yes, **man.**
   - Which word has the middle sound **ĕĕĕ?**
     (Signal.) *Men.* Yes, **men.**

━━━━━ **EXERCISE 3** ━━━━━

e

NEW **VOWEL VARIATIONS**

1. (Point to **e:**) One sound you learned for
   this letter is the letter name. Everybody,
   what's the sound? (Touch.) *ēēē.*
2. What's the other sound? (Touch.) *ĕĕĕ.*
3. (Point to **e:**) In some words this letter
   makes the sound **ēēē.** In other words it
   makes the sound **ĕĕĕ.**
4. (Point to the underlined part of **she.**
   Pause.) What sound in this word?
   (Touch.) *ēēē.*
   - (Touch the ball of the arrow for **she.**
     Pause.) What word? (Slash right:) *She.*
5. (Repeat step 4 for **them, shed, hen, feet,
   seem, he, hem.**)
6. (Repeat the list until the students can
   correctly identify all the words in order.)

she

them

shed

hen

feet

seem

he

hem

EXERCISE 4

WORD READING THE FAST WAY

1. You're going to read these words the fast way.
2. (Touch the ball of the arrow for **had**. Pause 4 seconds.) What word? (Slash right:) *Had.*
3. (Touch the ball for **hod**. Pause 4 seconds.) What word? (Slash right:) *Hod.*
4. (Touch the ball for **hid**. Pause 4 seconds.) What word? (Slash right:) *Hid.*
5. (Repeat step 4 for remaining words.)

had

hod

hid

heed

rid

reed

rod

mod

mad

mid

nods

shot

hash

cons

cans

fast

sing

his

WORKBOOK EXERCISES

Note: Pass out the Workbooks. Direct the students to open to Lesson 26.

(Award 6 points if the group worked well during the word attack. Remind the students of the points they can earn in their Workbook.)

EXERCISE 5

NEW SPELLING FROM DICTATION

1. Touch part 1 in your Workbook. ✓
• You're going to write words in the blanks as I dictate them.
2. First word: **cat.** What word? (Signal.) *Cat.*
• **Cat** has three sounds. I'll say **cat** a sound at a time. Listen: **c . . . ăăă . . . t.**
• Listen again: **c . . . ăăă . . . t.**
3. Your turn. Say the sounds in **cat.** Get ready. (Clap three times:) *c . . . ăăă . . . t.*
4. Write the word **cat** in the first blank. (Observe students and give feedback.)

> **To correct:**
> a. Say the sounds in **cat.** Get ready.
> b. Show me the letter for **c.** ✓
> • Show me the letter for **ăăă.** ✓
> • Show me the letter for **t.** ✓

5. Next word: **did.** What word? (Signal.) *Did.*
• I'll say **did** a sound at a time. Listen: **d . . . ĭĭĭ . . . d.**
6. Your turn. Say the sounds in **did.** Get ready. (Clap three times:) *d . . . ĭĭĭ . . . d.*
7. Write the word **did** in the next blank. (Observe students and give feedback.)
8. (Repeat steps 5–7 for **dad, she.**)

Lesson 26 **47**

EXERCISE 6

WORD COMPLETION

1. Everybody, touch the first line in part 2 in your Workbook. ✓
2. You're going to write the word (pause) **an** on the first line. What word? (Signal.) *An.* Yes, **an.**
• Write (pause) **an** on the first line. (Observe students and give feedback.)
3. Now you're going to change (pause) **an** to say (pause) **man.**
• Listen: **man.** What is the first sound in (pause) **man?** (Signal.) *mmm.* Yes, **mmm.**
• Fix it up to say **man.** (Observe students and give feedback.)
4. Listen. You started with a word. What word? (Signal.) *An.* Yes, **an.**
• What word do you have now? (Signal.) *Man.* Yes, **man.**
5. Touch the second line. ✓
• You're going to write the word (pause) **in.** What word? (Signal.) *In.* Yes, **in.**
• Write (pause) **in** on the line. (Observe students and give feedback.)

Lesson 26 **185**

6. Now you're going to change (pause) **in** to say (pause) **sin.**
- Listen: **sin.** What is the first sound in (pause) **sin?** (Signal.) *sss.* Yes, **sss.**
- Fix it up to say **sin.**
(Observe students and give feedback.)
7. Listen. You started with a word. What word? (Signal.) *In.*
- What word do you have now? (Signal.) *Sin.* Yes, **sin.**
8. Touch the third line. ✓
- You're going to write the word (pause) **it.** What word? (Signal.) *It.* Yes, **it.**
- Write (pause) **it** on the line.
(Observe students and give feedback.)
9. Now you're going to change (pause) **it** to say (pause) **sit.**
- Listen: **sit.** What is the first sound in (pause) **sit?** (Signal.) *sss.* Yes, **sss.**
- Fix it up to say **sit.**
(Observe students and give feedback.)
10. Listen. You started with a word. What word? (Signal.) *It.*
- What word do you have now? (Signal.) *Sit.* Yes, **sit.**

━━━━━━━ **EXERCISE 7** ━━━━━━━
SOUND DICTATION

1. I'll say the sounds. You write the letters in part 3 in your Workbook.
2. First sound. (Pause.) **ĕĕĕ.** What sound? (Signal.) *ĕĕĕ.*
- Write it in the first blank.
(Observe students and give feedback.)
3. Next sound. (Pause.) **nnn.** What sound? (Signal.) *nnn.*
- Write it.
(Observe students and give feedback.)
4. (Repeat step 3 for **t, shshsh, ŏŏŏ, g, ĭĭĭ, h, ĕĕĕ, ēēē, mmm, ăăă.**)
5. (Repeat sounds students had trouble with.)

━━━━━━━ **EXERCISE 8** ━━━━━━━
WORD READING: Workbook

1. Touch the first word in part 4.
- Tell me the sound for the underlined part. Then tell me the word.
2. Touch the underlined sound in the first word. (Pause.) What sound? (Signal.) *ēēē.*
- (Pause.) What word? (Signal.) *Sheets.*
3. Touch the underlined sound in the next word. (Pause.) What sound? (Signal.) *ĭĭĭ.*
- (Pause.) What word? (Signal.) *Fits.*
4. (Repeat step 3 for **ca̱ts, ham̱s, fa̱st, dam̱, di̱n, see̱s, maṯs, fee̱d, da̱n, fee̱t, di̱m, sha̱d, fee̱s.**)

━━━━━━━ **EXERCISE 9** ━━━━━━━
NEW **SENTENCE READING**

Task A

1. Everybody, touch part 5. ✓
2. Touch under the first word. ✓
- What word? (Signal.) *She.*
3. Next word. ✓
- What word? (Signal.) *Did.*
4. (Repeat steps 3 for **not, see, him.**)
5. (Repeat steps 2–4 until the students can correctly identify all the words in the sentence in order.)
6. (Repeat steps 2–5 for each remaining sentence:
- **2. That fish has a fin.**
- **3. A cat had sand on his feet.**
- **4. She hid in the hen shed.**)

Individual test
Everybody, point to the first word in sentence 1. (Call on a student.) Take your time. See if you can read all the words in this sentence the fast way without making a mistake. Everybody else, touch under the words that are read. (Give each student a chance to read one of the sentences.)

Task B

1. Everybody, touch sentence 3. ✓
• I'll read that sentence. Follow along. **A cat had sand on his feet.**
2. Here are some questions:
   a. Everybody, what did the cat have on his feet? (Signal.) *Sand.*
   b. Where was the sand? (Call on a student.) (Idea: *On the cat's feet.*)

EXERCISE 10
WORD COMPLETION

1. Everybody, touch part 6. ✓
2. Sound out the word on the first line. Get ready. (Clap for **th, i:**) *ththth̄īĭ.*
• What word? (Signal.) *thi.* Yes, **thi.**
3. Fix it up to say (pause) **this.** (Pause.) **This.** What word? (Signal.) *This.* Yes, **this.**
• Fix it up.
   (Observe students and give feedback.)
4. Sound out the word on the next line. Get ready. (Clap for **r, a, t:**) *rrrăăăt.*
• What word? (Signal.) *Rat.* Yes, **rat.**
5. Fix it up to say (pause) **rats.** (Pause.) **Rats.** What word? (Signal.) *Rats.* Yes, **rats.**
• Fix it up.
   (Observe students and give feedback.)
6. Sound out the word on the third line. Get ready. (Clap for **h, i:**) *hīĭĭ.*
• What word? (Signal.) *hi.* Yes, **hi.**
7. Fix it up to say (pause) **him.** (Pause.) **Him.** What word? (Signal.) *Him.* Yes, **him.**
• Fix it up.
   (Observe students and give feedback.)
8. Sound out the word on the fourth line. Get ready. (Clap for **sh, o:**) *shshsh̄ŏŏŏ.*
• What word? (Signal.) *shŏ.* Yes, **shŏ.**
9. Fix it up to say (pause) **shot.** (Pause.) **Shot.** What word? (Signal.) *Shot.* Yes, **shot.**
• Fix it up.
   (Observe students and give feedback.)

Individual test
I'll call on different students to read words. First word. (Call on a student.) What word? (Call on different students to read the remaining words.)

EXERCISE 11
MATCHING COMPLETION

1. Everybody, touch part 7. ✓
• Read the words the fast way.
2. Touch under the first word. ✓
• What word? (Signal.) *Hot.*
3. Next word. ✓
• What word? (Signal.) *Hits.*
4. (Repeat step 3 for **shot, mad, sheet, hats.**)
5. Later, you're going to write the words in the second column.

EXERCISE 12
CIRCLE GAME

1. Everybody, touch part 8. ✓
2. What will you circle in the first two lines? (Signal.) *nnn.*
3. What will you circle in the next two lines? (Signal.) *g.*
4. What will you circle in the last two lines? (Signal.) *d.*
5. Circle the sounds and finish the rest of your Workbook lesson.

EXERCISE 13
WORKBOOK CHECK

1. (Check each student's Workbook.)
2. (Award points for Workbook performance.)
3. (Record the student's total points in Box B.)

0–2 errors	8 points
3–4 errors	4 points
5–6 errors	2 points
7 or more errors	0 points

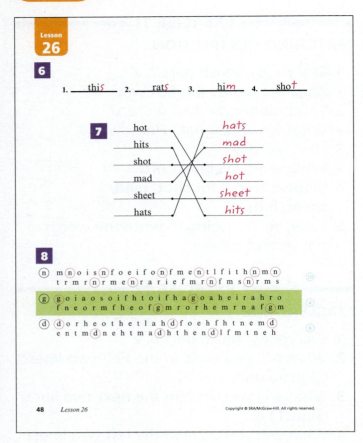

INDIVIDUAL READING CHECKOUTS

EXERCISE 14

SENTENCE-READING CHECKOUT

- Study the sentences in part 5. You'll each get a turn to read all these sentences. You can earn as many as 6 points for this reading.
- If you read all the sentences with no more than 1 error, you'll earn 6 points.
- If you make more than 1 error, you do not earn any points. But you'll have another chance to earn 6 points by studying the sentences some more and reading them again.
- (Check the students individually.)
- (Record either 6 or 0 points in Box C.)

Lesson point total

(Tell students to write the point total in the last box at the top of the Workbook page. Maximum for the lesson = 20 points.)

Point Summary Chart

(Tell students to write this point total in the box for Lesson 26 in the Point Summary Chart.)

END OF LESSON 26

WORD-ATTACK SKILLS

e

VOWEL VARIATIONS

1. (Point to **e:**) One sound you learned for this letter is the letter name. Everybody, what's that sound? (Touch.) *ēēē.*
2. What's the other sound? (Touch.) *ĕĕĕ.*
3. (Point to **e:**) In some words this letter makes the sound *ēēē.* In other words it makes the sound *ĕĕĕ.*
4. (Touch the ball of the arrow for **end.** Pause.) What sound in this word? (Touch.) *ĕĕĕ.*
- (Point to the beginning of **end.** Pause.) What word? (Slash right:) *End.*
5. (Repeat step 4 for **send, mend, me, sent, tent.**)
6. (Repeat the list until the students can correctly identify all the words in order.)

EXERCISE 1
NEW SOUND INTRODUCTION

1. (Point to **c:**) This letter makes the sound **k.** What sound? (Touch.) *k.* Yes, **k.**
2. (Point to **k:**) This letter also makes the sound **k.** What sound? (Touch.) *k.* Yes, **k.**
3. (Point to **ck:**) These letters also make the sound **k.** What sound? (Touch.) *k.* Yes, **k.**
4. (Point to **e:**) One sound you learned for this letter is the letter name. Everybody, what's that sound? (Touch.) *ēēē.* Yes, *ēēē.*
- What's the other sound? (Touch.) *ĕĕĕ.* Yes, **ĕĕĕ.**
5. Say each sound when I touch it.
6. (Point to **i:**) What sound? (Touch.) *ĭĭĭ.* Yes, *ĭĭĭ.*
7. (Repeat step 6 for **r, sh, th, g, ing, ŏ, ă.**)

c k ck
e i r
sh th g
ing o a

Individual test
I'll call on different students to say all the sounds. If everybody I call on can say all the sounds without making a mistake, we'll go on to the next exercise. (Call on two or three students. Touch under each sound. Each student says all the sounds, including two sounds for **e.**)

end
send
mend
me
sent
tent

7. (Touch the ball of the arrow for **teen**. Pause.) **What sound in this word?** (Touch.) *ēēē.*
   - (Point to the beginning of **teen**. Pause.) **What word?** (Slash right:) *Teen.*
8. (Repeat step 7 for **m̲eet, m̲et, te̲n, h̲em**.)
9. (Repeat the list until the students can correctly identify all the words in order.)

teen

m̲eet

m̲et

te̲n

h̲em

━━━━━━ **EXERCISE 3** ━━━━━━
PRONUNCIATIONS

> **Note:** Do not write the words on the board. This is an oral exercise.

Task A

1. Listen. He **fell** down the hill. (Pause.) **Fell.** Say it. (Signal.) *Fell.*
2. Next word. Listen. I **feel** sick. (Pause.) **Feel.** Say it. (Signal.) *Feel.*
3. Next word. Listen. Will you **fill** my cup? (Pause.) **Fill.** Say it. (Signal.) *Fill.*

4. Next word: **rims.** Say it. (Signal.) *Rims.*
5. (Repeat step 4 for **mast, mats.**)
6. (Repeat all the words until firm.)

Task B   Him, hem

1. Listen: **him.** Say it. (Signal.) *Him.*
2. Get ready to tell me the middle sound. Listen: **hǐǐǐmmm.** What's the middle sound? (Signal.) *ǐǐǐ.* Yes, **ǐǐǐ.**
3. Listen: **hem.** Say it. (Signal.) *Hem.*
4. Get ready to tell me the middle sound. Listen: **hěěěmmm.** What's the middle sound? (Signal.) *ěěě.* Yes, **ěěě.**
5. One of those words has the middle sound **ǐǐǐ.** I'll say the words again: **him** (pause) **hem.** Which word has the middle sound **ǐǐǐ?** (Signal.) *Him.* Yes, **him.**
6. Which word has the middle sound **ěěě?** (Signal.) *Hem.* Yes, **hem.**

Task C   Pill, pal, peel

1. Listen. She swallowed a **pill.** (Pause.) **Pill.** Say it. (Signal.) *Pill.*
2. Get ready to tell me the middle sound. Listen: **pǐǐǐlll.** What's the middle sound? (Signal.) *ǐǐǐ.* Yes, **ǐǐǐ.**
3. Listen. Tom is my **pal.** (Pause.) **Pal.** Say it. (Signal.) *Pal.*
4. Get ready to tell me the middle sound. Listen: **pǎǎǎlll.** What's the middle sound? (Signal.) *ǎǎǎ.* Yes, **ǎǎǎ.**
5. Listen: **peel.** Say it. (Signal.) *Peel.*
6. Get ready to tell me the middle sound. Listen: **pēēēlll.** What's the middle sound? (Signal.) *ēēē.* Yes, **ēēē.**
7. One of those words has the middle sound **ǐǐǐ.** I'll say the words again: **pill, pal, peel.** Which word has the middle sound **ǐǐǐ?** (Signal.) *Pill.* Yes, **pill.**
8. Which word has the middle sound **ǎǎǎ?** (Signal.) *Pal.* Yes, **pal.**
9. Which word has the middle sound **ēēē?** (Signal.) *Peel.* Yes, **peel.**

EXERCISE 4
WORD READING THE FAST WAY

1. You're going to read these words the fast way.
2. (Touch the ball of the arrow for **sad**. Pause 4 seconds.) What word? (Slash right:) *Sad.*
3. (Touch the ball for **sid**. Pause 4 seconds.) What word? (Slash right:) *Sid.*
4. (Touch the ball for **seed**. Pause 4 seconds.) What word? (Slash right:) *Seed.*
5. (Repeat step 4 for remaining words.)

sad

sid

seed

sod

hit

hat

hot

dan

don

din

cash

cats

mats

mast

ring

his

WORKBOOK EXERCISES

> **Note:** Pass out the Workbooks. Direct the students to open to Lesson 27.

(Award 6 points if the group worked well during the word attack. Remind the students of the points they can earn in their Workbook.)

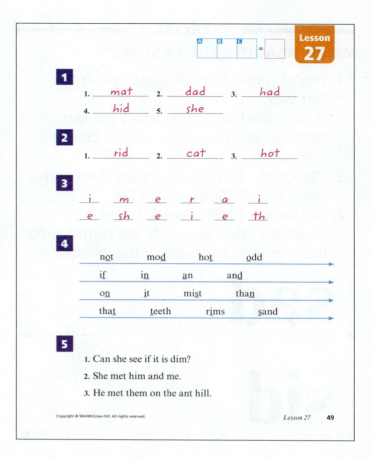

--- **EXERCISE 5** ---

SPELLING FROM DICTATION

1. Touch part 1 in your Workbook. ✓
• You're going to write words in the blanks as I dictate them.
2. First word: **mat.** What word? (Signal.) *Mat.*
• **Mat** has three sounds. I'll say **mat** one sound at a time. Listen: **mmm . . . ăăă . . . t.**
• Listen again: **mmm . . . ăăă . . . t.**
3. Your turn. Say the sounds in **mat.** Get ready. (Clap three times:) *mmm . . . ăăă . . . t.*
4. Write the word **mat** in the first blank. (Observe students and give feedback.)

> **To correct:**
> a. Say the sounds in **mat.** Get ready.
> b. Show me the letter for **m.** ✓
> • Show me the letter for **ăăă.** ✓
> • Show me the letter for **t.** ✓

5. Next word: **dad.** What word? (Signal.) *Dad.*
• I'll say **dad** a sound at a time. Listen: **d . . . ăăă . . . d.**
6. Your turn. Say the sounds in **dad.** Get ready. (Clap three times:) *d . . . ăăă . . . d.*
7. Write the word **dad** in the next blank. (Observe students and give feedback.)
8. (Repeat steps 5–7 for **had, hid, she.**)

--- **EXERCISE 6** ---

WORD COMPLETION

1. Everybody, touch the first line in part 2 in your Workbook. ✓
2. You're going to write the word (pause) **id** on the first line. What word? (Signal.) *id.* Yes, **id.**
• Write (pause) **id** on the first line. (Observe students and give feedback.)
3. Now you're going to change (pause) **id** to say (pause) **rid.**
• Listen: **rid.** What is the first sound in (pause) **rid?** (Signal.) *rrr.* Yes, **rrr.**
• Fix it up to say **rid.** (Observe students and give feedback.)
4. Listen. You started with a word. What word? (Signal.) *id.* Yes, **id.**
• What word do you have now? (Signal.) *Rid.* Yes, **rid.**
5. Touch the next line. ✓
• You're going to write the word (pause) **at.** What word? (Signal.) *At.* Yes, **at.**
• Write (pause) **at** on the line. (Observe students and give feedback.)

6. Now you're going to change (pause) **at** to say (pause) **cat.**
- Listen: **cat.** What is the first sound in (pause) **cat?** (Signal.) *c.* Yes, **c.**
- Fix it up to say **cat.**
(Observe students and give feedback.)
7. Listen. You started with a word. What word? (Signal.) *At.*
- What word do you have now? (Signal.) *Cat.* Yes, **cat.**
8. Touch the next line. ✓
- You're going to write the word (pause) **ot.** What word? (Signal.) *ot.* Yes, **ot.**
- Write (pause) **ot** on the line.
(Observe students and give feedback.)
9. Now you're going to change (pause) **ot** to say (pause) **hot.**
- Listen: **hot.** What is the first sound in (pause) **hot?** (Signal.) *h.* Yes, **h.**
- Fix it up to say **hot.**
(Observe students and give feedback.)
10. Listen. You started with a word. What word? (Signal.) *ot.*
- What word do you have now? (Signal.) *Hot.* Yes, **hot.**

━━━━━━ **EXERCISE 7** ━━━━━━

SOUND DICTATION

1. I'll say the sounds. You write the letters in part 3 in your Workbook.
2. First sound. (Pause.) **ĭĭĭ.** What sound? (Signal.) *ĭĭĭ.*
- Write it in the first blank.
(Observe students and give feedback.)
3. Next sound. (Pause.) **mmm.** What sound? (Signal.) *mmm.*
- Write it.
(Observe students and give feedback.)
4. (Repeat step 3 for **ĕĕĕ, rrr, ăăă, ĭĭĭ, ēēē, shshsh, ēēē, ĭĭĭ, ĕĕĕ, thththth.**)
5. (Repeat sounds students had trouble with.)

━━━━━━ **EXERCISE 8** ━━━━━━

NEW ▶ **WORD READING: Workbook**

1. Touch the first word in part 4. ✓
2. Tell me the underlined sound in the first word. (Pause.) What sound? (Signal.) *ŏŏŏ.*
- (Pause.) What word? (Signal.) *Not.*
3. Next word. (Pause.) What sound? (Signal.) *d.*
- (Pause.) What word? (Signal.) *Mod.*
4. (Repeat step 3 for **ho̱t, o̱dd, i̱f, i̱n, a̱n, aṉd, o̱n, i̱t, mi̱st, tha̱n, tha̱t, tee̱th, ri̱ms, s̱and.**)

━━━━━━ **EXERCISE 9** ━━━━━━

NEW ▶ **SENTENCE READING**

Task A

1. Everybody, touch part 5. ✓
2. Sentence 1 has a question mark at the end because that sentence asks a question. Touch the question mark. ✓
3. Touch under the first word in sentence 1. ✓
- What word? (Signal.) *Can.*
4. Next word. ✓
- What word? (Signal.) *She.*
5. (Repeat step 4 for **see, if, it, is, dim.**)
6. (Repeat steps 3–5 until the students can correctly identify all the words in the sentence in order.)
7. (Repeat steps 3–6 for each remaining sentence:
- **2. She met him and me.**
- **3. He met them on the ant hill.**)

┌─────────────────────────────────┐
Individual test
Everybody, point to the first word in sentence 1. (Call on a student.) Take your time. See if you can read all the words in this sentence the fast way without making a mistake. Everybody else, touch under the words that are read. (Give each student a chance to read one of the sentences.)
└─────────────────────────────────┘

Task B

1. Everybody, touch sentence 3. ✓
• I'll read that sentence. Follow along. **He
met them on the ant hill.**
2. Here are some questions:
   a. Everybody, where did he meet them?
      (Signal.) *On the ant hill.*
   b. What is an ant hill? (Call on a student.
      Accept a reasonable response.)
   c. Everybody, did he meet one person or
      more than one person? (Signal.) *More
      than one person.*

=========== **EXERCISE 10** ===========

WORD COMPLETION

1. Everybody, touch part 6. ✓
2. Sound out the word on the first line. Get
   ready. (Clap for **f, i:**) *fffĭĭĭ.*
• What word? (Signal.) *fi.* Yes, **fi.**
3. Fix it up to say (pause) **fit.** (Pause.) **Fit.**
   What word? (Signal.) *Fit.* Yes, **fit.**
• Fix it up.
   (Observe students and give feedback.)
4. Sound out the word on the next line. Get
   ready. (Clap for **f, i:**) *fffĭĭĭ.*
• What word? (Signal.) *fi.* Yes, **fi.**
5. Fix it up to say (pause) **fits.** (Pause.) **Fits.**
   What word? (Signal.) *Fits.* Yes, **fits.**
• Fix it up.
   (Observe students and give feedback.)
6. Sound out the word on the third line. Get
   ready. (Clap for **th, i:**) *thththĭĭĭ.*
• What word? (Signal.) *thi.* Yes, **thi.**
7. Fix it up to say (pause) **this.** (Pause.) **This.**
   What word? (Signal.) *This.* Yes, **this.**
• Fix it up.
   (Observe students and give feedback.)
8. Sound out the word on the fourth line.
   Get ready. (Clap for **th, a:**) *thththăăă.*
• What word? (Signal.) *tha.* Yes, **tha.**
9. Fix it up to say (pause) **that.** (Pause.) **That.**
   What word? (Signal.) *That.* Yes, **that.**
• Fix it up.
   (Observe students and give feedback.)

Individual test
I'll call on different students to read
words in part 6. First word. (Call on a
student.) What word? (Call on different
students to read the remaining words.)

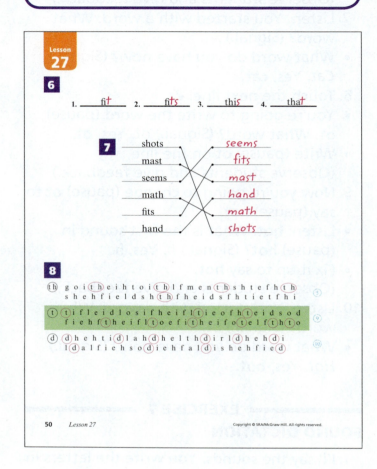

EXERCISE 11
MATCHING COMPLETION

1. Everybody, touch part 7. ✓
• Read the words the fast way.
2. Touch under the first word. ✓
• What word? (Signal.) *Shots.*
3. Next word. ✓
• What word? (Signal.) *Mast.*
4. (Repeat step 3 for **seems, math, fits, hand.**)
5. Later, you're going to write the words in the second column.

EXERCISE 12
CIRCLE GAME

1. Everybody, touch part 8. ✓
2. What will you circle in the first two lines? (Signal.) *ththth.*
3. What will you circle in the next two lines? (Signal.) *t.*
4. What will you circle in the last two lines? (Signal.) *d.*
5. Circle the sounds and finish the rest of your Workbook lesson.

EXERCISE 13
WORKBOOK CHECK

1. (Check each student's Workbook.)
2. (Award points for Workbook performance.)
3. (Record the student's total points in Box B.)

0–2 errors	8 points
3–4 errors	4 points
5–6 errors	2 points
7 or more errors	0 points

INDIVIDUAL READING CHECKOUTS

EXERCISE 14
SENTENCE-READING CHECKOUT

• Study the sentences in part 5. You'll each get a turn to read all these sentences. You can earn as many as 6 points for this reading.
• If you read all the sentences with no more than 1 error, you'll earn 6 points.
• If you make more than 1 error, you do not earn any points. But you'll have another chance to earn 6 points by studying the sentences some more and reading them again.
• (Check the students individually.)
• (Record either 6 or 0 points in Box C.)

Lesson point total

(Tell students to write the point total in the last box at the top of the Workbook page. Maximum for the lesson = 20 points.)

Point Summary Chart

(Tell students to write this point total in the box for Lesson 27 in the Point Summary Chart.)

END OF LESSON 27

WORD-ATTACK SKILLS

SOUND INTRODUCTION

1. (Point to **c:**) This letter makes the sound **k**. What sound? (Touch.) *k*. Yes, **k**.
2. (Point to **k:**) This letter also makes the sound **k**. What sound? (Touch.) *k*. Yes, **k**.
3. (Point to **ck:**) These letters also make the sound **k**. What sound? (Touch.) *k*. Yes, **k**.
4. (Point to **e:**) One sound you learned for this letter is the letter name. Everybody, what's that sound? (Touch.) *ēēē*. Yes, **ēēē**.
- What's the other sound? (Touch.) *ēēē*. Yes, **ĕĕĕ**.
5. Say each sound when I touch it.
6. (Point to **a:**) What sound? (Touch.) *ăăă*. Yes, **ăăă**.
7. (Repeat step 6 for **ing, ĭ, g, d, ŏ, th**.)

c k ck
e a ing
i g d
o th

Individual test
I'll call on different students to say all the sounds. If everybody I call on can say all the sounds without making a mistake, we'll go on to the next exercise. (Call on two or three students. Touch under each sound. Each student says all the sounds, including two sounds for **e**.)

e

VOWEL VARIATIONS

1. (Point to **e:**) One sound you learned for this letter is the letter name. Everybody, what's the sound? (Touch.) *ēēē*.
2. What's the other sound? (Touch.) *ĕĕĕ*.
3. (Point to **e:**) In some words this letter makes the sound **ēēē**. In other words it makes the sound **ĕĕĕ**.
4. (Touch the ball of the arrow for **teen**. Pause.) What sound in this word? (Touch.) *ēēē*.
- (Point to the beginning of **teen**. Pause.) What word? (Slash right:) *Teen*.
5. (Repeat step 4 for **ten, meet, met**.)
6. (Repeat the list until the students can correctly identify all the words in order.)

t<u>ee</u>n
t<u>e</u>n
m<u>ee</u>t
m<u>e</u>t

7. (Touch the ball of the arrow for **me.** Pause.) What sound in this word? (Touch.) ēēē.
- (Point to the beginning of **me.** Pause.) What word? (Slash right:) *Me.*
8. (Repeat step 7 for the following list.)
9. (Repeat the list until the students can correctly identify all the words in order.)

me ●————————————→

men ●————————————→

see ●————————————→

sent ●————————————→

send ●————————————→

mend ●————————————→

tent ●————————————→

end ●————————————→

———————— **EXERCISE 3** ————————
PRONUNCIATIONS

> **Note:** Do not write the words on the board. This is an oral exercise.

Task A **Fill, fell**

1. Listen: **fill.** Say it. (Signal.) *Fill.*
2. Get ready to tell me the middle sound. Listen: **fffĭĭĭlll.** What's the middle sound? (Signal.) ĭĭĭ. Yes, ĭĭĭ.
3. Listen: **fell.** Say it. (Signal.) *Fell.*
4. Get ready to tell me the middle sound. Listen: **fffĕĕĕlll.** What's the middle sound? (Signal.) ĕĕĕ. Yes, ĕĕĕ.
5. One of those words has the middle sound ĭĭĭ. I'll say the words again: **fill** (pause) **fell.** Which word has the middle sound ĭĭĭ? (Signal.) *Fill.* Yes, **fill.**
6. Which word has the middle sound ĕĕĕ? (Signal.) *Fell.* Yes, **fell.**

Task B **Feel, fell**

1. Listen: **feel.** Say it. (Signal.) *Feel.*
2. Get ready to tell me the middle sound. Listen: **fffēēēlll.** What's the middle sound? (Signal.) ēēē. Yes, ēēē.
3. Listen: **fell.** Say it. (Signal.) *Fell.*
4. Get ready to tell me the middle sound. Listen: **fffĕĕĕlll.** What's the middle sound? (Signal.) ĕĕĕ. Yes, ĕĕĕ.
5. One of those words has the middle sound ēēē. I'll say the words again: **feel** (pause) **fell.** Which word has the middle sound ēēē? (Signal.) *Feel.* Yes, **feel.**
6. Which word has the middle sound ĕĕĕ? (Signal.) *Fell.* Yes, **fell.**

Task C **Mid, mad, mod**

1. Listen: **mid.** Say it. (Signal.) *Mid.*
2. Get ready to tell me the middle sound. Listen: **mmmĭĭĭd.** What's the middle sound? (Signal.) ĭĭĭ. Yes, ĭĭĭ.
3. Listen: **mad.** Say it. (Signal.) *Mad.*
4. Get ready to tell me the middle sound. Listen: **mmmăăăd.** What's the middle sound? (Signal.) ăăă. Yes, ăăă.

5. Listen: **mod.** Say it. (Signal.) *Mod.*

6. Get ready to tell me the middle sound. Listen: **mmmŏŏŏd.** What's the middle sound? (Signal.) *ŏŏŏ.* Yes, **ŏŏŏ.**

7. One of those words has the middle sound **ĭĭĭ.** I'll say the words again: **mid, mad, mod.** Which word has the middle sound **ĭĭĭ?** (Signal.) *Mid.* Yes, **mid.**

8. Which word has the middle sound **ăăă?** (Signal.) *Mad.* Yes, **mad.**

9. Which word has the middle sound **ŏŏŏ?** (Signal.) *Mod.* Yes, **mod.**

Task D **Men, man**

1. Listen. There are two **men.** (Pause.) **Men.** Say it. (Signal.) *Men.*

• Listen. There is one **man.** (Pause.) **Man.** Say it. (Signal.) *Man.*

2. One of those words has the middle sound **ĕĕĕ.** I'll say the words again: **men, man.** Which word has the middle sound **ĕĕĕ?** (Signal.) *Men.* Yes, **men.**

3. Which word has the middle sound **ăăă?** (Signal.) *Man.* Yes, **man.**

EXERCISE 4

NEW **WORD READING THE FAST WAY**

1. You're going to read these words the fast way.

2. (For each word: Touch the ball of the arrow. Pause.) What word? (Slash right.)

3. (Repeat each list until firm.)

sheets

shots

got

on

in

an

teeth

tin

mast

sing

his

cot

cots

4. (For each word: Touch the ball of the arrow. Pause.) What word? (Slash right.)
5. (Repeat the column until firm.)

not

needs

dams

mash

gash

WORKBOOK EXERCISES

Note: Pass out the Workbooks. Direct the students to open to Lesson 28.

(Award 6 points if the group worked well during the word attack. Remind the students of the points they can earn in their Workbook.)

EXERCISE 5
NEW SPELLING FROM DICTATION

1. Touch part 1 in your Workbook. ✓
• You're going to write words that I dictate.
2. First word: **the.** What word? (Signal.) *The.*
• Listen again: **ththth . . . ēēē.** Write it in the first blank.
(Observe students and give feedback.)

To correct:
a. Say the sounds in **the.** Get ready.
b. Show me the letters for **ththth.** ✓
• Show me the letter for **ēēē.** ✓

3. Next word: **see.** What word? (Signal.) *See.*
• Listen again: **sss . . . ēēē.** Write it in the next blank. Remember to write two **ē**'s.
(Observe students and give feedback.)
4. (Repeat step 3 for **she, did, hid.**)

EXERCISE 6
WORD COMPLETION

1. Everybody, touch the first line in part 2 in your Workbook. ✓
2. You're going to write the word (pause) **eet** on the first line. What word? (Signal.) *eet.* Yes, **eet.**
• Write (pause) **eet** on the first line.
(Observe students and give feedback.)
3. Now you're going to change (pause) **eet** to say (pause) **feet.**
• Listen: **feet.** What is the first sound in (pause) **feet?** (Signal.) *fff.* Yes, **fff.**
• Fix it up to say **feet.**
(Observe students and give feedback.)

4. Listen. You started with a word. What word? (Signal.) *eet.* Yes, **eet.**

- What word do you have now? (Signal.) *Feet.* Yes, **feet.**

5. Touch the next line. ✓

- You're going to write the word (pause) **ad.** What word? (Signal.) *Ad.* Yes, **ad.**

- Write (pause) **ad** on the line. (Observe students and give feedback.)

6. Now you're going to change (pause) **ad** to say (pause) **sad.**

- Listen: **sad.** What is the first sound in (pause) **sad?** (Signal.) *sss.* Yes, **sss.**

- Fix it up to say **sad.** (Observe students and give feedback.)

7. Listen. You started with a word. What word? (Signal.) *Ad.*

- What word do you have now? (Signal.) *Sad.* Yes, **sad.**

8. Touch the next line. ✓

- You're going to write the word (pause) **od.** What word? (Signal.) *od.* Yes, **od.**

- Write (pause) **od** on the line. (Observe students and give feedback.)

9. Now you're going to change (pause) **od** to say (pause) **rod.**

- Listen: **rod.** What is the first sound in (pause) **rod?** (Signal.) *rrr.* Yes, **rrr.**

- Fix it up to say **rod.** (Observe students and give feedback.)

10. Listen. You started with a word. What word? (Signal.) *od.*

- What word do you have now? (Signal.) *Rod.* Yes, **rod.**

Workbook page 51

A	B	C		
Lesson 28

1
1. the   2. see   3. she
4. did   5. hid

2
1. feet   2. sad   3. rod

3
(c   k)   ck   e   n   r
e   a   th   i   sh   o

4
teen	hand	kiss	keen	kin
sand	meek	seek	sick	mint
got	gash	dim	rim	deed

5
1. He had cash in his hand.
2. Did she see the deed?
3. Ten wet rats sat in the mash.

Lesson 28   51

EXERCISE 7

NEW **SOUND DICTATION**

1. I'll say the sounds. You write the letters in part 3 in your Workbook.

2. First sound. Write a letter that says **k** in the first blank. (Observe students and give feedback.)

3. Next sound. Write another letter that says **k**. (Observe students and give feedback.)

4. Next sound. Write two letters that go together and say **k**. (Observe students and give feedback.)

5. Next sound. (Pause.) **ĕĕĕ.** What sound? (Signal.) *ĕĕĕ.*

- Write it. (Observe students and give feedback).

6. (Repeat step 5 for **nnn, rrr, ēēē, ăăă, ththth, ĭĭĭ, shshsh, ŏŏŏ.**)

7. (Repeat sounds students had trouble with.)

EXERCISE 8

WORD READING: Workbook

1. Touch the first word in part 4. ✓
2. Tell me the underlined sound in the first word. (Pause.) What sound? (Signal.) ēēē.
- (Pause.) What word? (Signal.) *Teen.*
3. Next word. (Pause.) What sound? (Signal.) *nnn.*
- (Pause.) What word? (Signal.) *Hand.*
4. (Repeat step 3 for remaining words.)

EXERCISE 9

SENTENCE READING

Task A

1. Everybody, touch part 5. ✓
2. Touch the first word in sentence 1. ✓
- What word? (Signal.) *He.*
3. Next word. ✓
- What word? (Signal.) *Had.*
4. (Repeat step 3 for **cash, in, his, hand.**)
5. Sentence 2 has a question mark at the end because that sentence asks a question. Touch the question mark at the end of sentence 2. ✓
6. Touch the first word in sentence 2. ✓
- What word? (Signal.) *Did.*
7. Next word. ✓
- What word? (Signal.) *She.*
8. (Repeat step 7 for **see, the, deed.**)
9. (Repeat steps 6–8 for sentence 3: **Ten wet rats sat in the mash.**)

> **Individual test**
> Everybody, point to the first word in sentence 1. (Call on a student.) Take your time. See if you can read all the words in this sentence the fast way without making a mistake. Everybody else, touch under the words that are read. (Give each student a chance to read one of the sentences.)

Task B

1. Everybody, touch sentence 1. ✓
- I'll read that sentence. Follow along. **He had cash in his hand.**
2. Here are some questions:
   a. Everybody, what did he have in his hand? (Signal.) *Cash.*
   b. What is cash? (Call on a student. Accept a reasonable response.)
   c. Would you like to have cash in your hand? (Call on a student.)

EXERCISE 10

WORD COMPLETION

1. Everybody, touch part 6. ✓
2. Tell me the sound on the first line. Get ready. (Clap for **th:**) *ththth.*
3. Fix it up to say (pause) **that.** (Pause.) **That.** What word? (Signal.) *That.* Yes, **that.**
- Fix it up.
  (Observe students and give feedback.)
4. Tell me the sound on the second line. Get ready. (Clap for **th:**) *ththth.*
5. Fix it up to say (pause) **this.** (Pause.) **This.** What word? (Signal.) *This.* Yes, **this.**
- Fix it up.
  (Observe students and give feedback.)
6. Tell me the sound on the third line. Get ready. (Clap for **th:**) *ththth.*
7. Fix it up to say (pause) **than.** (Pause.) **Than.** What word? (Signal.) *Than.* Yes, **than.**
- Fix it up.
  (Observe students and give feedback.)
8. Tell me the sound on the fourth line. Get ready. (Clap for **th:**) *ththth.*
9. Fix it up to say (pause) **them.** (Pause.) **Them.** What word? (Signal.) *Them.* Yes, **them.**
- Fix it up.
  (Observe students and give feedback.)

> **Individual test**
> I'll call on different students to read words in part 6. First word. (Call on a student.) What word? (Call on different students to read the remaining words.)

Lesson 28

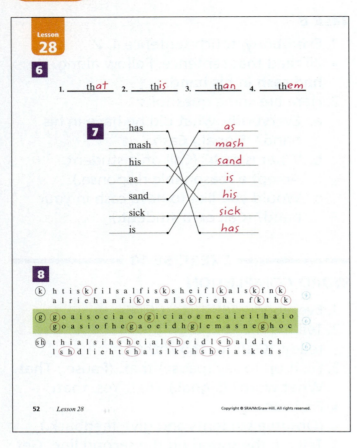

6
1. th*at*   2. th*is*   3. th*an*   4. th*em*

7
has   *as*
mash   *mash*
his   *sand*
as   *is*
sand   *his*
sick   *sick*
is   *has*

8
(k) h t i s (k) f i l s a l f i s (k) s h e i f l (k) a l s (k) f n (k)
a l r i e h a n f i (k) e n a l s (k) f i e h t n f (k) t h (k)

(g) g o a i s o c i a o o (g) i c i a o e m c a i e i t h a i o
(g) o a s i o f h e (g) a o e i d h (g) l e m a s n e (g) h o c

(sh) t h i a l s i h (sh) e i a l (sh) e i d l (sh) a l d i e h
l (sh) d l i e h t (sh) a l s l k e h (sh) e i a s k e h s

52   *Lesson 28*   Copyright © SRA/McGraw-Hill. All rights reserved.

EXERCISE 11
MATCHING COMPLETION

1. Everybody, touch part 7. ✓
- Read the words the fast way.
2. Touch under the first word. ✓
- What word? (Signal.) *Has.*
3. Next word. ✓
- What word? (Signal.) *Mash.*
4. (Repeat step 3 for **his, as, sand, sick, is.**)
5. Later, you're going to write the words in the second column.

EXERCISE 12
CIRCLE GAME

1. Everybody, touch part 8. ✓
2. What will you circle in the first two lines? (Signal.) *k.*
3. What will you circle in the next two lines? (Signal.) *g.*
4. What will you circle in the last two lines? (Signal.) *shshsh.*
5. Circle the sounds and finish the rest of your Workbook lesson.

EXERCISE 13
WORKBOOK CHECK

1. (Check each student's Workbook.)
2. (Award points for Workbook performance.)
3. (Record the student's total points in Box B.)

0–2 errors	8 points
3–4 errors	4 points
5–6 errors	2 points
7 or more errors	0 points

INDIVIDUAL READING CHECKOUTS

EXERCISE 14
SENTENCE-READING CHECKOUT

- Study the sentences in part 5. You'll each get a turn to read all these sentences. You can earn as many as 6 points for this reading.
- If you read all the sentences with no more than 1 error, you'll earn 6 points.
- If you make more than 1 error, you do not earn any points. But you'll have another chance to earn 6 points by studying the sentences some more and reading them again.
- (Check the students individually.)
- (Record either 6 or 0 points in Box C.)

Lesson point total

(Tell students to write the point total in the last box at the top of the Workbook page. Maximum for the lesson = 20 points.)

Point Summary Chart

(Tell students to write this point total in the box for Lesson 28 in the Point Summary Chart.)

END OF LESSON 28

WORD-ATTACK SKILLS

SOUND IDENTIFICATION

1. (Point to **e:**) One sound you learned for this letter is the letter name. Everybody, what's that sound? (Touch.) *ēēē*. Yes, **ēēē**.
- What's the other sound? (Touch.) *ĕĕĕ*. Yes, **ĕĕĕ**.
2. Say each sound when I touch it.
3. (Point to **c:**) What sound? (Touch.) *k*. Yes, **k**.
4. (Repeat step 3 for **ck, th, ă, sh, ĭ, ŏ, g**.)

e c ck
th a sh
i o g

> **Individual test**
> I'll call on different students to say all the sounds. If everybody I call on can say all the sounds without making a mistake, we'll go on to the next exercise. (Call on two or three students. Touch under each sound. Each student says all the sounds, including two sounds for **e**.)

e

VOWEL VARIATIONS

1. (Point to **e:**) One sound you learned for this letter is the letter name. Everybody, what's that sound? (Touch.) *ēēē*.
2. What's the other sound? (Touch.) *ĕĕĕ*.
3. (Point to **e:**) In some words this letter makes the sound **ēēē**. In other words it makes the sound **ĕĕĕ**.
4. (Point to the underlined part of **end**. Pause.) What sound in this word? (Touch.) *ĕĕĕ*.
- (Touch the ball of the arrow for **end**. Pause.) What word? (Slash right:) *End*.
5. (Repeat step 4 for **red, sheet, seen, tree**.)
6. (Repeat the list until the students can correctly identify all the words in order.)

end

red

sheet

seen

tree

7. (Point to the underlined part of **get**.
Pause.) What sound in this word?
(Touch.) ĕĕĕ.
• (Touch the ball of the arrow for **get**.
Pause.) What word? (Slash right:) *Get.*
8. (Repeat step 7 for the remaining words in
the column.)
9. (Repeat the list until the students can
correctly identify all the words in order.)

get

ten

tend

tent

dent

met

meet

teeth

PRONUNCIATIONS

> **Note:** Do not write the words on the
> board. This is an oral exercise.

Task A Ten, tin, tan

1. Listen: **ten.** Say it. (Signal.) *Ten.*
2. Next word. Listen. The can was made of
tin. (Pause.) **Tin.** Say it. (Signal.) *Tin.*
3. Next word. Listen. The dog was black and
tan. (Pause.) **Tan.** Say it. (Signal.) *Tan.*
4. (Repeat all the words until firm.)

Task B Sit, set

1. Listen. **Sit** next to me. (Pause.) **Sit.** Say it.
(Signal.) *Sit.*
• Listen. He **set** the table. (Pause.) **Set.** Say
it. (Signal.) *Set.*
2. One of those words has the middle sound
ĭĭĭ. I'll say the words again: sit (pause) set.
3. Which word has the middle sound ĭĭĭ?
(Signal.) *Sit.* Yes, **sit.**
• Which word has the middle sound ĕĕĕ?
(Signal.) *Set.* Yes, **set.**

Task C Pot, pet

1. Listen: **pot** (pause) **pet.** Say those words.
(Signal.) *Pot, pet.* (Repeat until firm.)
2. One of those words has the middle sound
ŏŏŏ. I'll say the words again: **pot**
(pause) **pet.**
• Which word has the middle sound ŏŏŏ?
(Signal.) *Pot.* Yes, **pot.**
3. Which word has the middle sound ĕĕĕ?
(Signal.) *Pet.* Yes, **pet.**

EXERCISE 4

WORD READING THE FAST WAY

1. You're going to read these words the fast way.
2. (For each word: Touch the ball of the arrow. Pause.) What word? (Slash right.)
3. (Repeat each list until firm.)

sag

rag

tags

fig

fin

fit

fist

fits

ant

hand

cash

fast

hold

rot

on

if

4. (For each word: Touch the ball of the arrow. Pause.) What word? (Slash right.)
5. (Repeat the column until firm.)

add

odd

cons

hits

WORKBOOK EXERCISES

Note: Pass out the Workbooks. Direct the students to open to Lesson 29.

(Award 6 points if the group worked well during the word attack. Remind the students of the points they can earn in their Workbook.)

EXERCISE 5
SPELLING FROM DICTATION

1. Touch part 1 in your Workbook. ✓
• You're going to write words that I dictate.
2. First word: **this.** What word? (Signal.) *This.*
• Listen again: **ththth . . . ĭĭĭ . . . sss.** Write it in the first blank.
(Observe students and give feedback.)

To correct:
a. Say the sounds in **this.** Get ready.
b. Show me the letters for **ththth.** ✓
• Show me the letter for **ĭĭĭ.** ✓
• Show me the letter for **sss.** ✓

3. Next word: **the.** What word? (Signal.) *The.*
• Listen again: **ththth . . . ēēē.** Write it in the next blank.
(Observe students and give feedback.)
4. (Repeat step 3 for **that, he, she, dad.**)

EXERCISE 6
WORD COMPLETION

1. Everybody, touch the first line in part 2 in your Workbook. ✓
2. You're going to write the word (pause) **eet** on the first line. What word? (Signal.) *eet.* Yes, **eet.**
• Write (pause) **eet** on the first line. Remember to write two **ē**'s.
(Observe students and give feedback.)

3. Now you're going to change (pause) **eet** to say (pause) **meet.**

- Listen: **meet.** What is the first sound in (pause) **meet?** (Signal.) *mmm.* Yes, **mmm.**
- Fix it up to say **meet.**
  (Observe students and give feedback.)

4. Listen. You started with a word. What word? (Signal.) *eet.* Yes, **eet.**

- What word do you have now? (Signal.) *Meet.* Yes, **meet.**

5. Touch the second line. ✓

- You're going to write the word (pause) **id.** What word? (Signal.) *id.* Yes, **id.**
- Write (pause) **id** on the line.
  (Observe students and give feedback.)

6. Now you're going to change (pause) **id** to say (pause) **did.**

- Listen: **did.** What is the first sound in (pause) **did?** (Signal.) *d.* Yes, **d.**
- Fix it up to say **did.**
  (Observe students and give feedback.)

7. Listen. You started with a word. What word? (Signal.) *id.*

- What word do you have now? (Signal.) *Did.* Yes, **did.**

8. Touch the third line. ✓

- You're going to write the word (pause) **am.** What word? (Signal.) *Am.* Yes, **am.**
- Write (pause) **am** on the line.
  (Observe students and give feedback.)

9. Now you're going to change (pause) **am** to say (pause) **ham.**

- Listen: **ham.** What is the first sound in (pause) **ham?** (Signal.) *h.* Yes, **h.**
- Fix it up to say **ham.**
  (Observe students and give feedback.)

10. Listen. You started with a word. What word? (Signal.) *Am.*

- What word do you have now? (Signal.) *Ham.* Yes, **ham.**

1
1. this 2. the 3. that
4. he 5. she 6. dad

2
1. meet 2. did 3. ham

3
(c   k)   ck   i   o   e
f   s   sh   e   th   t

4
did   dad   deed   mint   sheets
fins   kiss   kit   ash   odd   sod
sin   sash   seems   math   mash

5
1. Can she sit on ten tan mats?
2. An ant is not fast in the dash.
3. She got sand and ants in the dish.

Lesson 29   53

———— EXERCISE 7 ————

SOUND DICTATION

1. I'll say the sounds. You write the letters in part 3 in your Workbook.
2. First sound. Write a letter that says **k** in the first blank.
   (Observe students and give feedback.)
3. Next sound. Write another letter that says **k.**
   (Observe students and give feedback.)
4. Next sound. Write two letters that go together and say **k.**
   (Observe students and give feedback.)
5. Next sound. (Pause.) $\bar{\imath}\bar{\imath}\bar{\imath}$. What sound? (Signal.) $\bar{\imath}\bar{\imath}\bar{\imath}$.

- Write it.
  (Observe students and give feedback).

6. (Repeat step 5 for **ŏŏŏ, ēēē, fff, sss, shshsh, ĕĕĕ, ththth, t.**)
7. (Repeat sounds students had trouble with.)

Lesson 29   **207**

===== **EXERCISE 8** =====

WORD READING: Workbook

1. Touch the first word in part 4. ✓
2. Tell me the underlined sound in the first word. (Pause.) What sound? (Signal.) ĭĭĭ.
• (Pause.) What word? (Signal.) *Did.*
3. Next word. (Pause.) What sound? (Signal.) ăăă.
• (Pause.) What word? (Signal.) *Dad.*
4. (Repeat step 3 for each remaining word.)

===== **EXERCISE 9** =====

SENTENCE READING

Task A

1. Everybody, touch part 5. ✓
2. Touch the first word in sentence 1. ✓
• What word? (Signal.) *Can.*
3. Next word. ✓
• What word? (Signal.) *She.*
4. (Repeat step 3 for **sit, on, ten, tan, mats.**)
5. (Repeat steps 2–4 until the students can correctly identify all the words in the sentence in order.)
6. (Repeat steps 2–5 for each remaining sentence:
• **2. An ant is not fast in the dash.**
• **3. She got sand and ants in the dish.**)

> **Individual test**
> Everybody, point to the first word in sentence 1. (Call on a student.) Take your time. See if you can read all the words in this sentence the fast way without making a mistake. Everybody else, touch under the words that are read. (Give each student a chance to read one of the sentences.)

Task B

1. Everybody, touch sentence 2. ✓
• I'll read that sentence. Follow along. **An ant is not fast in the dash.**

2. Here are some questions:
   a. Everybody, who is not fast in the dash? (Signal.) *An ant.*
   b. What is a dash? (Call on a student.) (Idea: *A short race.*)
   c. Why isn't an ant fast in the dash? (Call on a student. Accept a reasonable response.)

===== **EXERCISE 10** =====

WORD COMPLETION

1. Everybody, touch part 6. ✓
2. Sound out the word on the first line. Get ready. (Clap for **f, i:**) fffĭĭĭ.
• What word? (Signal.) *fi.* Yes, **fi.**
3. Fix it up to say (pause) **fins.** (Pause.) **Fins.** What word? (Signal.) *Fins.* Yes, **fins.**
• Fix it up.
(Observe students and give feedback.)
4. Tell me the sound on the next line. Get ready. (Clap for **th:**) ththth.
5. Fix it up to say (pause) **that.** (Pause.) **That.** What word? (Signal.) *That.* Yes, **that.**
• Fix it up.
(Observe students and give feedback.)
6. Sound out the word on the third line. Get ready. (Clap for **r, a:**) rrrăăă.
• What word? (Signal.) *ra.* Yes, **ra.**
7. Fix it up to say (pause) **rams.** (Pause.) **Rams.** What word? (Signal.) *Rams.* Yes, **rams.**
• Fix it up.
(Observe students and give feedback.)
8. Sound out the word on the fourth line. Get ready. (Clap for **h, a:**) hăăă.
• What word? (Signal.) *ha.* Yes, **hă.**
9. Fix it up to say (pause) **hats.** (Pause.) **Hats.** What word? (Signal.) *Hats.* Yes, **hats.**
• Fix it up.
(Observe students and give feedback.)

> **Individual test**
> I'll call on different students to read words in part 6. First word. (Call on a student.) What word? (Call on different students to read the remaining words.)

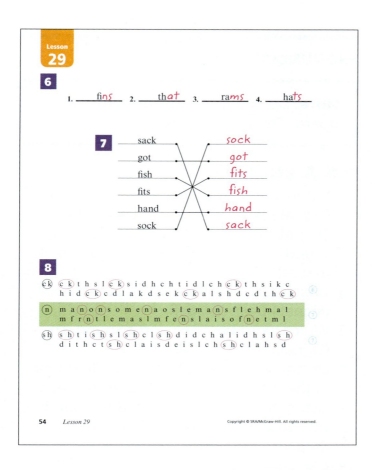

EXERCISE 11
MATCHING COMPLETION

1. Everybody, touch part 7. ✓
- Read the words the fast way.
2. Touch under the first word. ✓
- What word? (Signal.) *Sack.*
3. Next word. ✓
- What word? (Signal.) *Got.*
4. (Repeat step 3 for **fish, fits, hand, sock.**)
5. Later, you're going to write the words in the second column.

EXERCISE 12
CIRCLE GAME

1. Everybody, touch part 8. ✓
2. What will you circle in the first two lines? (Signal.) *ck.*
3. What will you circle in the next two lines? (Signal.) *nnn.*
4. What will you circle in the last two lines? (Signal.) *shshsh.*
5. Circle the sounds and finish the rest of your Workbook lesson.

EXERCISE 13
WORKBOOK CHECK

1. (Check each student's Workbook.)
2. (Award points for Workbook performance.)
3. (Record the student's total points in Box B.)

0–2 errors	8 points
3–4 errors	4 points
5–6 errors	2 points
7 or more errors	0 points

INDIVIDUAL READING CHECKOUTS

EXERCISE 14
SENTENCE-READING CHECKOUT

- Study the sentences in part 5. You'll each get a turn to read all these sentences. You can earn as many as 6 points for this reading.
- If you read all the sentences with no more than 1 error, you'll earn 6 points.
- If you make more than 1 error, you do not earn any points. But you'll have another chance to earn 6 points by studying the sentences some more and reading them again.
- (Check the students individually.)
- (Record either 6 or 0 points in Box C.)

Lesson point total
(Tell students to write the point total in the last box at the top of the Workbook page. Maximum for the lesson = 20 points.)

Point Summary Chart
(Tell students to write this point total in the box for Lesson 29 in the Point Summary Chart.)

END OF LESSON 29

WORD-ATTACK SKILLS

EXERCISE 1
SOUND IDENTIFICATION

1. (Point to **e**:) One sound you learned for this letter is the letter name. Everybody, what's that sound? (Touch.) ēēē. Yes, ēēē.
- What's the other sound? (Touch.) ĕĕĕ. Yes, ĕĕĕ.
2. Say each sound when I touch it.
3. (Point to **ing**:) What sound? (Touch.) ing. Yes, **ing**.
4. (Repeat step 3 for **th, ă, ĭ, ŏ, sh, s, r, d, h, m, n.**)

e ing
th a i
o sh s
r d h
m n

Individual test
(Call on two or three students. Touch under each sound. Each student says all the sounds, including two sounds for **e**.)

EXERCISE 2
PRONUNCIATIONS

Note: Do not write the words on the board. This is an oral exercise.

***Task A* Bell, bill**

1. Listen: **bell** (pause) **bill.** Say those words. (Signal.) *Bell, bill.* (Repeat until firm.)
2. One of those words has the middle sound ĕĕĕ. I'll say the words again: **bell** (pause) **bill.**
- Which word has the middle sound ĕĕĕ? (Signal.) *Bell.* Yes, **bell.**
3. Which word has the middle sound ĭĭĭ? (Signal.) *Bill.* Yes, **bill.**
4. Listen: **bĕĕĕlll.** What's the middle sound in the word **bell?** (Signal.) ĕĕĕ. Yes, ĕĕĕ.
- Listen: **bĭĭĭlll.** What's the middle sound in the word **bill?** (Signal.) ĭĭĭ. Yes, ĭĭĭ. (Repeat until firm.)

***Task B* Din, den**

1. Listen: **din** (pause) **den.** Say those words. (Signal.) *Din, den.* (Repeat until firm.)
2. One of those words has the middle sound ĭĭĭ. I'll say the words again: **din** (pause) **den.**
- Which word has the middle sound ĭĭĭ? (Signal.) *Din.* Yes, **din.**
3. Which word has the middle sound ĕĕĕ? (Signal.) *Den.* Yes, **den.**
4. Listen: **dĭĭĭnnn.** What's the middle sound in the word **din?** (Signal.) ĭĭĭ. Yes, ĭĭĭ.
- Listen: **dĕĕĕnnn.** What's the middle sound in the word **den?** (Signal.) ĕĕĕ. Yes, ĕĕĕ.
5. (Repeat step 4 until firm.) Good job.

***Task C* Fill, fell**

1. Listen: **fill** (pause) **fell.** Say those words. (Signal.) *Fill, fell.* (Repeat until firm.)
2. One of those words has the middle sound ĕĕĕ. I'll say the words again: **fill** (pause) **fell.**
- Which word has the middle sound ĕĕĕ? (Signal.) *Fell.* Yes, **fell.**

3. Which word has the middle sound ĭĭĭ?
   (Signal.) *Fill.* Yes, **fill.**
4. Listen: **fĭĭĭlll.** What's the middle sound in
   the word **fill?** (Signal.) *ĭĭĭ.* Yes, **ĭĭĭ.**
- Listen: **fĕĕĕlll.** What's the middle sound in
  the word **fell?** (Signal.) *ĕĕĕ.* Yes, **ĕĕĕ.**
5. (Repeat step 4 until firm.) Good job.

Task D Bean, ben, ban

1. Listen: **bean, ben, ban.** Say those words.
   (Signal.) *Bean, ben, ban.*
   (Repeat until firm.)
2. One of those words has the middle
   sound **ăăă.** I'll say the words again: **bean,
   ben, ban.**
- Which word has the middle sound **ăăă?**
  (Signal.) *Ban.* Yes, **ban.**
3. Which word has the middle sound **ēēē?**
   (Signal.) *Bean.* Yes, **bean.**
- Which word has the middle sound **ĕĕĕ?**
  (Signal.) *Ben.* Yes, **ben.**
4. Listen: **bēēēnnn.** What's the middle
   sound in the word **bean?** (Signal.) *ēēē.*
   Yes, **ēēē.**
- Listen: **bĕĕĕnnn.** What's the middle
  sound in the word **ben?** (Signal.) *ĕĕĕ.*
  Yes, **ĕĕĕ.**
- Listen: **băăănnn.** What's the middle
  sound in the word **ban?** (Signal.) *ăăă.*
  Yes, **ăăă.**
5. (Repeat step 4 until firm.) Good job.

EXERCISE 3

e

VOWEL VARIATIONS

1. (Point to **e:**) One sound you learned for
   this letter is the letter name. Everybody,
   what's that sound? (Touch.) *ēēē.*
2. What's the other sound? (Touch.) *ĕĕĕ.*
3. (Point to **e:**) In some words this letter
   makes the sound **ēēē.** In other words it
   makes the sound **ĕĕĕ.**

4. (Point to the underlined part of **hen.**
   Pause.) What sound in this word?
   (Touch.) *ĕĕĕ.*
- (Touch the ball of the arrow for **hen.**
  Pause.) What word? (Slash right:) *Hen.*
5. (Repeat step 4 for all words in the column.)
6. (Repeat the list until the students can
   correctly identify all the words in order.)

hen

then

he

get

she

leg

teeth

m**e**t

r**e**d

sent

f**e**d

f**ee**d

WORD READING THE FAST WAY

1. You're going to read these words the fast way.
2. (For each word: Touch the ball of the arrow. Pause.) What word? (Slash right.)
3. (Repeat each list until firm. Lists continue on next page.)

heed

hid

had

his

has

hand

met

ten

sag

teen

sit

sad

sacks

socks

on

rocks

Note: Pass out the Workbooks. Direct the students to open to Lesson 30.

(Award 6 points if the group worked well during the word attack. Remind the students of the points they can earn in their Workbook.)

EXERCISE 5
SPELLING FROM DICTATION

1. Touch part 1 in your Workbook. ✓
• You're going to write words that I dictate.
2. First word: **she.** What word? (Signal.) *She.*
• Listen again: **shshsh . . . ēēē.** Write it in the first blank.
   (Observe students and give feedback.)

> **To correct:**
> a. Say the sounds in **she.** Get ready.
> b. Show me the letters for **shshsh.** ✓
> • Show me the letter for **ēēē.** ✓

3. Next word: **that.** What word?
   (Signal.) *That.*
• Listen again: **thththt . . . ăăă . . . t.** Write it in the next blank.
   (Observe students and give feedback.)
4. (Repeat step 3 for **he, had, mad, hid.**)

Lesson 30

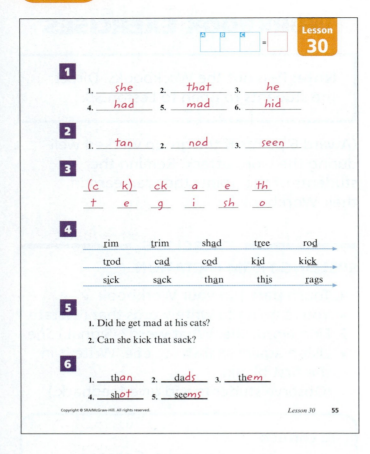

6. Now you're going to change (pause) **od** to say (pause) **nod.**
- Listen: **nod.** What is the first sound in (pause) **nod?** (Signal.) *nnn.* Yes, **nnn.**
- Fix it up to say **nod.** (Observe students and give feedback.)
7. Listen. You started with a word. What word? (Signal.) *od.*
- What word do you have now? (Signal.) *Nod.* Yes, **nod.**
8. Touch the third line. ✓
- You're going to write the word (pause) **een.** What word? (Signal.) *een.* Yes, **een.**
- Write (pause) **een** on the line. Remember to write two ē's. (Observe students and give feedback.)
9. Now you're going to change (pause) **een** to say (pause) **seen.**
- Listen: **seen.** What is the first sound in (pause) **seen?** (Signal.) *sss.* Yes, **sss.**
- Fix it up to say **seen.** (Observe students and give feedback.)
10. Listen. You started with a word. What word? (Signal.) *een.*
- What word do you have now? (Signal.) *Seen.* Yes, **seen.**

EXERCISE 7
SOUND DICTATION

1. I'll say the sounds. You write them in part 3 on your Workbook page.
2. First sound. Write a letter that says **k** in the first blank. (Observe students and give feedback.)
3. Next sound. Write another letter that says **k.** (Observe students and give feedback.)
4. Next sound. Write two letters that go together and say **k.** (Observe students and give feedback.)
5. Next sound. (Pause.) *ăăă.* What sound? (Signal.) *ăăă.*
- Write it. ✓
6. (Repeat step 5 for **ēēē, ththth, t, ēēē, g, ĭĭĭ, shshsh, ŏŏŏ.**)
7. (Repeat sounds students had trouble with.)

EXERCISE 6
WORD COMPLETION

1. Everybody, touch the first line in part 2 in your Workbook. ✓
2. You're going to write the word (pause) **an** on the first line. What word? (Signal.) *An.* Yes, **an.**
- Write (pause) **an** on the first line. (Observe students and give feedback.)
3. Now you're going to change (pause) **an** to say (pause) **tan.**
- Listen: **tan.** What is the first sound in (pause) **tan?** (Signal.) *t.* Yes, **t.**
- Fix it up to say **tan.** (Observe students and give feedback.)
4. Listen. You started with a word. What word? (Signal.) *An.* Yes, **an.**
- What word do you have now? (Signal.) *Tan.* Yes, **tan.**
5. Touch the second line. ✓
- You're going to write the word (pause) **od.** What word? (Signal.) *od.* Yes, **od.**
- Write (pause) **od** on the line. (Observe students and give feedback.)

214 *Lesson 30*

EXERCISE 8

WORD READING: Workbook

1. Touch the first word in part 4. ✓
2. Tell me the underlined sound in the first word. (Pause.) What sound? (Signal.) *rrr.*
- (Pause.) What word? (Signal.) *Rim.*
3. Next word. (Pause.) What sound? (Signal.) *t.*
- (Pause.) What word? (Signal.) *Trim.*
4. (Repeat step 3 for **shad, tree, rod, trod, cad, cod, kid, kick, sick, sack, than, this, rags.**)

EXERCISE 9

NEW SENTENCE READING

Task A

1. Everybody, touch part 5. ✓
2. Touch under the first word. ✓
- What word? (Signal.) *Did.*
3. Next word. ✓
- What word? (Signal.) *He.*
4. (Repeat step 3 for **get, mad, at, his, cats.**)
5. (Repeat steps 2–4 until the students can correctly identify all the words in the sentence in order.)
6. (Repeat steps 2–5 for sentence 2: **Can she kick that sack?**)

> **Individual test**
> (Give each student a chance to read one of the sentences.)

EXERCISE 10

WORD COMPLETION

1. Everybody, touch part 6. ✓
2. Tell me the sound on the first line. Get ready. (Clap for **th:**) *ththth.*
3. Fix it up to say (pause) **than.** (Pause.) **Than.** What word? (Signal.) *Than.* Yes, **than.**
- Fix it up.
  (Observe students and give feedback.)
4. Sound out the word on the next line. Get ready. (Clap for **d, a:**) *dăăă.*
- What word? (Signal.) *da.* Yes, **da.**

5. Fix it up to say (pause) **dads.** (Pause.) **Dads.** What word? (Signal.) *Dads.* Yes, **dads.**
- Fix it up.
  (Observe students and give feedback.)
6. Tell me the sound on the next line. Get ready. (Clap for **th:**) *ththth.*
7. Fix it up to say (pause) **them.** (Pause.) **Them.** What word? (Signal.) *Them.* Yes, **them.**
- Fix it up.
  (Observe students and give feedback.)
8. Tell me the sound on the fourth line. Get ready. (Clap for **sh:**) *shshsh.*
9. Fix it up to say (pause) **shot.** (Pause.) **Shot.** What word? (Signal.) *Shot.* Yes, **shot.**
- Fix it up.
  (Observe students and give feedback.)
10. Sound out the word on the fifth line. Get ready. (Clap for **s, ee:**) *sssēēē.*
- What word? (Signal.) *See.* Yes, **see.**
11. Fix it up to say (pause) **seems.** (Pause.) **Seems.** What word? (Signal.) *Seems.* Yes, **seems.**
- Fix it up.
  (Observe students and give feedback.)

> **Individual test**
> I'll call on different students to read words in part 6. First word. (Call on a student.) What word? (Call on different students to read the remaining words.)

EXERCISE 11

NEW STORY READING

Task A

1. Everybody, touch part 7. ✓
2. This is a story. There are pictures after some of the sentences. You're going to read the sentences the fast way.
3. Touch under the first word. ✓
- What word? (Signal.) *She.*
4. Next word. ✓
- What word? (Signal.) *Had.*
5. (Repeat step 4 for **3, fish.**)

> **To correct word-reading errors:**
> a. (Say the correct word.)
> b. What word? (Signal.)
> c. Everybody, back to the first word of the sentence. ✓
> d. (Repeat steps 3–5.)

6. (Repeat steps 3–5 for each remaining sentence:
- **This fish is a shad.**
- **This fish is a cod.**
- **This fish is in the cat.**)
7. (If the students miss more than four words, repeat the story reading from the beginning.)

Task B

1. Now I'll read the story and ask questions. Follow along.
2. **She had three fish.** Everybody, how many fish did she have? (Signal.) *Three.*
3. **This fish is a shad.** Touch the picture of the shad. ✓
4. **This fish is a cod.** Touch the picture of the cod. ✓
5. **This fish is in the cat.** I don't see the fish. Where is it? (Call on a student.) *In the cat.*
- How did it get in the cat? (Call on a student.) (Idea: *The cat ate it.*)
- Why does the cat look happy? (Call on a student.) (Accept a reasonable response.)

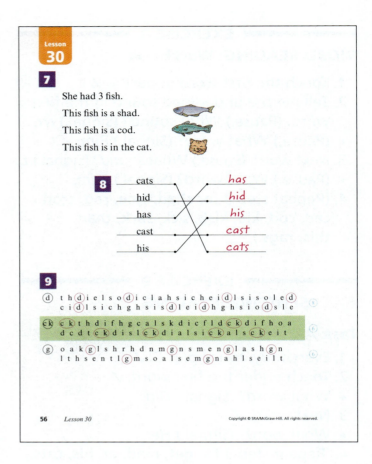

EXERCISE 12

MATCHING COMPLETION

1. Everybody, touch part 8. ✓
- Read the words the fast way.
2. Touch under the first word. ✓
- What word? (Signal.) *Cats.*
3. Next word. ✓
- What word? (Signal.) *Hid.*
4. (Repeat step 3 for **has, cast, his.**)
5. Later, you're going to write the words in the second column.

EXERCISE 13

CIRCLE GAME

1. Everybody, touch part 9. ✓
2. What will you circle in the first two lines? (Signal.) *d.*
3. What will you circle in the next two lines? (Signal.) *ck.*
4. What will you circle in the last two lines? (Signal.) *g.*
5. Circle the sounds and finish the rest of your Workbook lesson.

EXERCISE 14
WORKBOOK CHECK

1. (Check each student's Workbook.)
2. (Award points for Workbook performance.)
3. (Record the student's total points in Box B.)

0–2 errors	8 points
3–4 errors	4 points
5–6 errors	2 points
7 or more errors	0 points

INDIVIDUAL READING CHECKOUTS

EXERCISE 15
NEW **STORY-READING CHECKOUT**

- Study the story. If you read all the sentences with no more than 1 error, you'll earn 6 points.
- (Check the students individually.)
- (Record either 6 or 0 points in Box C.)

Lesson point total

(Tell students to write the point total in the last box at the top of the Workbook page. Maximum = 20 points.)

Point Summary Chart

(Tell students to write this point total in the box for Lesson 30 in the Point Summary Chart.)

Five-lesson point summary

(Tell students to add the point totals for Lessons 26 through 30 in the Point Summary Chart and to write the total for Block 6. Maximum for Block 6 = 100 points.)

END OF LESSON 30

MASTERY TEST 7
— AFTER LESSON 30, BEFORE LESSON 31 —

Note: Use students' Workbook part 1 Lesson 30 Sound dictation performance for part A of Mastery Test 7. Test each student individually on part B. Begin individual testing while students are completing their Workbook exercises. Administer the test so that other students do not overhear the student being tested.

Part A

(Use Sound dictation from Lesson 30, Exercise 7—Workbook Part 3.)

Part B Word reading the fast way

1. You're going to read these words the fast way. Read as carefully as you can.
2. (For each word, touch the ball of the arrow. Ask: What word? Slash right.)

Scoring the test

Part A Sound dictation from Workbook

1. (Count the number of errors each student made on Sound dictation in Lesson 30.)
- (Pass criterion: 0 or 1 error. Circle **P.**)
- (Fail criterion: 2 or more errors. Circle **F.**)
2. (Record **P** or **F** on the *Decoding A* Mastery Test Student Profile and Group Summary forms for Test 7.)

Part B Word reading

1. (Count the number of errors on Word reading, and record on the Student Profile and Group Summary forms.)
- (Pass criterion: 0 errors. Circle **P.**)
- (Fail criterion: 1 or more errors. Circle **F.**)

sent

cans

got

end

mast

dish

teeth

at

rod

kiss

Remedies

Part A Sound dictation

(For students who missed 2 or more sounds, repeat the sound-identification exercises in Lessons 29 and 30.)

Part B Word reading the fast way

(If more than 25 percent of the students missed any words, repeat Word reading the fast way in Lessons 26 and 30. Then retest.)